THE CASE FOR
Grace

Also by Lee Strobel

The Ambition (fiction)

The Case for Christ

The Case for Christianity Answer Book

The Case for Christmas

The Case for Christ Study Bible (general editor)

The Case for a Creator

The Case for Easter

The Case for Faith

The Case for the Real Jesus

Experiencing the Passion of Jesus (with Garry Poole)

Faith Under Fire: Exploring Christianity's Ten Toughest Questions
(with Garry Poole)

God's Outrageous Claims

Inside the Mind of Unchurched Harry and Mary

Surviving a Spiritual Mismatch in Marriage (with Leslie Strobel)

The Unexpected Adventure (with Mark Mittelberg)

What Jesus Would Say

THE CASE FOR

Grace

—

A Journalist Explores the Evidence of Transformed Lives

LEE STROBEL

NEW YORK TIMES BESTSELLING AUTHOR

 ZONDERVAN®
.com

WILLOW
Willow Creek Resources

ZONDERVAN

The Case for Grace
Copyright © 2015 by Lee Strobel

This title is also available as a Zondervan ebook.
Visit www.zondervan.com/ebooks.

Requests for information should be addressed to:
Zondervan, 3900 *Sparks Dr. SE, Grand Rapids, Michigan 49546*

ISBN 978-0-310-33618-1

International Trade Paper Edition

Cover design: Faceout Studio
Cover photography: Arti! / Getty Images®
Interior design: Beth Shagene

First printing January 2015 / Printed in the United States of America

For Abigail, Penelope,
Brighton, and Oliver—
God's gifts of grace

Therefore, if anyone is in Christ,
the new creation has come:
The old has gone, the new is here!

2 Corinthians 5:17

Contents

Preface

God's grace is the sole basis for both new life and spiritual vitality.

Stanley Grenz[1]

Defining grace can be as simple as one declarative sentence: "Grace is the favor shown by God to sinners."[2] From there, it can be expounded upon in volumes of theological treatises, but at its core it is an unmerited and unconditional gift of God's love that we can never earn or deserve.

Grace enables us to respond to God, enfolds us into his family, and empowers us to change. Theologian Thomas C. Oden said grace is necessary "to know truth, avoid sin, act well, pray fittingly, desire salvation, begin to have faith and persevere in faith."[3] Grace, he said, is nothing less than "the motivating power of the Christian life."[4]

Definitions are important, but this is not a textbook on grace. Instead, it is a collection of stories that illustrate the power of God to revolutionize human lives — to turn a homeless junkie into an ordained pastor; an adulterer into a marriage counselor; a reckless rebel into a selfless servant of God; and a mass murderer into a pardoned saint.

"Our past sins are not only forgiven (through Christ)," said Charles Colson, "but we are transformed to live a new life with God's power and grace."[5] Said Philip Yancey, "We can never sink so far that God's grace will not reach us. At the same time, grace does not leave us there. It raises us to new heights."[6]

This book describes a very personal journey for me, spawned by a crisis with my father, which sent me on a lifelong quest to solve the riddle of grace. Along the way, I found the undeniable evidence of grace in the life of a Korean orphan, shivering under straw in a foxhole; in a teenage addict in Amarillo, who didn't care whether his next injection would kill him; in a homeless felon in Las Vegas, scouring dumpsters for scraps of pizza crust; in a humiliated pastor in South Carolina, unmasked for his blatant hypocrisy; in the famous preacher's son who was living a wasted and vapid life in Boston; and in a Cambodian man who fled the Khmer Rouge, only to find his life intertwined with a notorious war criminal.

Each story contributes a piece to the grace puzzle, showing how grace goes beyond forgiveness to acceptance and even adoption by God; how it restores hope when none is left; how it extends to the most heinous circumstances; and how it allows us to forgive those who caused our most intimate wounds—and even to forgive ourselves. In other words, insights that all of us need.

As Christianity is unique among world religions, so is the grace Christ offers. Sometimes to understand grace we need to see it described rather than merely defined. After all, the Bible is one grand narrative about grace; when Jesus wanted his followers to fully feel the emotional impact of grace, he spun a parable about a Prodigal Son. "Jesus talked a lot about grace, but mainly through stories," said Yancey.[7]

So here are stories for you—true accounts of people whose transformation and renewal are so radical that they seem to be best explained as the work of a gracious God. Through them, I trust you will see your story playing out as well.

The Search for Grace

[God] waits to be wanted. Too bad that with many of us He waits so long, so very long, in vain.

A. W. Tozer[1]

He was leaning back in his leather recliner in the wood-paneled den, his eyes darting back and forth between the television set and me, as if he didn't deign to devote his full attention to our confrontation. In staccato bursts, he would lecture and scold and shout, but his eyes never met mine.

It was the evening before my high school graduation, and my dad had caught me lying to him—big-time.

Finally, he snapped his chair forward and shifted to look fully into my face, his eyes angry slits behind his glasses. He held up his left hand, waving his pinky like a taunt as he pounded each and every word: *"I don't have enough love for you to fill my little finger."*

He paused as the words smoldered. He was probably expecting me to fight back, to defend myself, to blubber or apologize or give in —at least to react in some way. But all I could do was to glare at him, my face flushed. Then after a few tense moments he sighed deeply, reclined again in his chair, and resumed watching TV.

That's when I turned my back on my father and strode toward the door.

I didn't need him. I was brash, I was driven and ambitious—I would slice my way through the world without his help. After all, I was about to make almost a hundred dollars a week at a summer job as a reporter for a rural newspaper in Woodstock, Illinois, and live on my own at a boarding house.

A plan formulated in my mind as I slammed the back door and began the trek toward the train station, lugging the duffel bag I had hurriedly packed. I would ask the newspaper to keep me on after the summer. Lots of reporters have succeeded without college, so why not me? Soon I'd make a name for myself. I'd impress the editors at the Chicago papers and eventually break into the big city. I'd ask my girlfriend to move in with me. I was determined to make it on my own —and never to go back home.

Someday, there would be payback. The day would come when my father would unfold the *Chicago Tribune* and his eye would catch my byline on a front-page exclusive. That would show him.

I was on a mission—and it was fueled by rage. But what I didn't realize as I marched down the gravel shoulder of the highway on that sultry June evening was that I was actually launching a far different quest than what I had supposed. It was a journey that I couldn't understand back then—and which would one day reshape my life in ways I never could have imagined.

That day I embarked on a lifelong pursuit of grace.

THE CASE FOR
Grace

CHAPTER 1

The Mistake

Someday You'll Understand

Psychoanalysis ... daily demonstrates to us how youthful persons lose their religious belief as soon as the authority of the father breaks down.

Sigmund Freud[1]

It wasn't until my mother was on her deathbed that she confirmed what years of therapy had only suggested to me: I was a mistake, at least in the eyes of my father.

My parents started with three children—first a girl, then two boys—and my dad threw himself into fatherhood. He coached his sons in Little League, led a Cub Scout troop, headed the high school boosters club, went on family vacations, and attended gymnastics meets and graduations.

Then after a lengthy time gap came the unexpected news that my mother was pregnant with me.

"Your dad was ... well, let's just say he was surprised," my mom told me in the waning weeks of her life, when we would chat for hours as she was bedridden with cancer. We had never broached this topic before, but we were in the midst of wonderfully candid conversations about our family's history, and I wanted to seize the opportunity to get some answers.

"Surprised how?"

She paused. "Not in a good way," she said, her eyes empathic.

"He was—what? Angry?"

"I don't want to say *angry*. Frustrated, yes. Upset by the circumstances. This just wasn't in his plans. And then I talked him into having another baby so you'd have a playmate." That was my younger sister.

This made sense to me. Years earlier, when I told my therapist about my relationship with my father — the emotional distance, the lack of engagement, the ongoing strife and flares of anger — he speculated that my inconvenient arrival in the family had interrupted my dad's plans for his future.

I could imagine my dad feeling that he had earned a respite after raising three kids. He was doing well financially, and I'm sure he wanted to travel and enjoy more freedom. Now at last was confirmation from my mother.

Our family lived in an upper-middle-class neighborhood northwest of Chicago. My dad worked hard to build his business, and he provided everything we needed — and more — materially. He was a faithful husband, well regarded in the community, and a committed friend to others.

Still, my relationship with him was always frosty. Maybe I needed more affirmation than the other kids, I don't know. But by the time I came along, there would be no Cub Scouts, no cheering at my Little League games, no watching my speech tournaments or attending my graduations. I can't think of a single in-depth conversation we ever had. I never heard the words I needed most.

Over time, I learned that the only way to gain his attention was through achievement. So I strived for good grades, was elected president of my junior high school, served as editor of the high school newspaper, and even wrote a column for the community paper. Still, none of the accolades satisfied. I don't remember any words of affection coming from my dad. Not one.

My parents were members of a Lutheran church; as a lawyer, my dad sat on the board of directors to offer free legal advice, although he was generally on the golf course on Sunday mornings.

I remember once when I was a youngster the entire family went to church together. After the service, my dad drove everyone home—but he forgot to bring me. I can still remember my panic as I searched frantically around the church, looking in vain for my father, my heart pounding.

It was an inadvertent mistake on his part, of course—but it was difficult for me not to see it as symbolic of how our relationship was developing.

Fathers and Faith

One evening when I was about twelve, my father and I clashed over something. I walked away feeling shame and guilt, and I went to bed vowing to try to behave better, to be more obedient, to somehow make myself more acceptable to my dad. I can't recall the details of what caused our conflict that evening, but what happened next is still vivid in my mind fifty years later.

I dreamed I was making myself a sandwich in the kitchen when a luminous angel suddenly appeared and started telling me about how wonderful and glorious heaven is. I listened for a while, then said matter-of-factly, "I'm going there"—meaning, of course, at the end of my life.

The angel's reply stunned me. "How do you know?"

How do I know? What kind of question is that? "Well, uh, I've tried to be a good kid," I stammered. "I've tried to do what my parents say. I've tried to behave. I've been to church."

Said the angel, "That doesn't matter."

Now I was staggered. How could it *not* matter—all my efforts to be compliant, to be dutiful, to live up to the demands of my parents and teachers. Panic rose in me. Words wouldn't come out of my mouth.

The angel let me stew for a few moments. Then he said, "Someday you'll understand." Instantly, he was gone—and I woke up in a sweat. It's the only dream I remember from my childhood. Periodically through the years it would come to mind, and yet I would always shake it off. It was just a dream.

As I got older, I found myself getting more confused about spiritual matters. When I became a teenager, my parents insisted that I attend confirmation classes at the church. "But I'm not sure I even believe that stuff," I told my dad. His response was stern: "Go. You can ask questions there."

The classes were built around rote memorization of the catechism; questions were only reluctantly tolerated and dealt with in a perfunctory way. I actually emerged with more doubts than when I started. I endured the process because when I was finally confirmed, the decision about whether to continue going to church would be mine—and I knew what the answer would be.

At the time I was oblivious to the fact that a young person's relationship with his father can greatly color his attitude toward God. I wasn't aware that many well-known atheists through history— including Friedrich Nietzsche, David Hume, Bertrand Russell, Jean-Paul Sartre, Albert Camus, Arthur Schopenhauer, Ludwig Feuerbach, Baron d'Holbach, Voltaire, H. G. Wells, Madalyn Murray O'Hair, and others—had felt abandoned or deeply disappointed with their fathers, making it less likely they would want to know a heavenly Father.[2]

I saw this illustrated later in life when I became friends with Josh McDowell, whose father was a violent alcoholic. "I grew up believing fathers hurt," Josh said. "People would tell me there's a heavenly Father who loves you. That didn't bring joy. It brought pain because I could not discern the difference between a heavenly Father and an earthly father." Josh became a self-described "ornery agnostic" until his investigation of Christianity convinced him it was true.[3]

Growing up, I just knew that as doubts festered inside and as my teachers insisted that science has eclipsed the need for God, I was being increasingly pulled toward skepticism. Something was missing—in my family and in my soul—that created a gnawing need I couldn't even describe at the time.

Years later I was driving down Northwest Highway in Palatine, Illinois—I can still recall the exact location, the time of day, the sunny weather—when I flipped the radio dial and heard something that flooded my eyes with tears.

I didn't catch it all, but it was about fathers and faith and God and hope. The voice belonged to someone who was born about the same time I was and yet whose life, in its astonishing horror and brutality, was the polar opposite of my own. Still, there was an instant connection, a bridge between us.

I had to track her down. I had to sit down and hear her story, one on one. I had to ask her my questions. Somehow I knew she held a piece to the puzzle of grace.

CHAPTER 2

The Orphan

God's Grace Goes Far beyond Forgiveness

> *Our understanding of Christianity cannot be*
> *better than our grasp of adoption.... Of all the*
> *gifts of grace, adoption is the highest.*
>
> J. I. Packer[1]

S tephanie Fast has never known her father. She suspects he was
an American soldier — possibly an officer — who fought in the
Korean conflict that started in 1950. There's even a chance he's still
alive somewhere. There's no way to tell.

I managed to track down Stephanie, that fleeting voice from the
radio, and flew from Denver to meet her in her tidy townhouse in a
wooded neighborhood in the Pacific Northwest. She's petite at five-
foot-three, her black hair falling in soft waves past her shoulders, her
almond eyes animated. Her husband, Darryl, a good-natured former
missionary, brought us some coffee but left us alone to chat in the
living room.

Stephanie is thoughtful as she begins to answer my questions, a
gentle Asian cadence in her voice. At times she looks off to the side, as
if reliving the experience she's struggling to describe. Other times she
leans forward to gesture with her hands, as if soliciting understanding.[2]

I settled into a chair opposite her. Looking for a place to start, I
said, "We were both born around the same time."

"I don't know exactly when or where I was born," she replied with
a shrug. "Possibly, it was in Pusan, since I was told I had an accent

21

from that region. But when? I don't know, although it was definitely in the same era as you."

"My earliest memory," I said, "was my third birthday. My grandparents in Florida gave me a wooden sailboat as a gift. But when we went back to Chicago, I accidently left it there. I was crushed." I chuckled at the thought. "Such are the traumas of a middle-class white kid growing up in suburban America in the fifties. I'm sure your earliest memory is much different. What's the first thing you recall?"

She thought for a moment and smiled. "I was about the same age —three or four," she replied. "It was the harvest festival in Korea, when family members come to the ancestral home. I remember all the fun—the sweets and games and wearing a beautiful dress—but I vividly recall my mom being so sad and sorrowful."

"Do you know why?"

"Well, that night I heard arguing between family members about the choice that she had to make for her future."

"What kind of choice?"

"After the Korean War there wasn't a place for biracial children in that country. That night, my mom was being given the option of a marriage—and I was not part of that option. Family members were saying that they had found a man who was willing to take her, but she couldn't bring me along. For her, the choice was, 'Do I want a future? If I do, then I can't have this child with me.' There was a lot of arguing and shame and guilt. I remember my mom crying and holding me all night."

"Was this because of discrimination against children born out of wedlock?"

"Yes, especially biracial ones. We were a reminder of an ugly war. I don't know the English word, but Koreans have a strong conviction of purity, and when I was younger I looked different from the other children. My hair and skin color were lighter, I had a crease in my eyes that most Koreans don't have, and I had wild, curly hair, which was quite unusual for Koreans. So people knew I was a half-breed."

"How did the family drama end?"

"At some point my mother reached her decision — she would entrust me to someone else. She told me I was going to my uncle's home. Within a few days, I remember walking down a dirt road to the city with her. It was the first time I ever heard a train. I asked her about it, and she said to me, 'That's where we're going.'

"When the train came, she got on board with me. Asians didn't have paper bags back then, so they would take a cloth about the size of a scarf and tie it together as a satchel. Inside I had a lunch and a couple of extra sets of clothing. She put it on a shelf above the seat, got on her knees, and told me, 'Don't be afraid.' She said I should get off the train with the other people, and my uncle would meet me. Then she left."

"What happened when you eventually got off the train?"

For a moment she didn't answer. She slowly shook her head.

"No one came for me."

"Garbage, Dust, Bastard, Alien Devil"

Here was a child not much older than a toddler, cast adrift in a frightening and dangerous place that was predisposed to reject her — a world without grace. "You must have been panic-stricken," I said.

"Not at first. I thought, *I'll stand here on the platform, and my uncle will come for me.* But when evening came, the trains stopped. The trainmaster came out and asked me what I was doing there. I told him I was waiting for my uncle — and that was the first time someone called me a *toogee*," she said, almost spitting out the epithet.

"What does that mean?"

"It's a very nasty word, like using the n-word today. It basically means half-breed or child of two bloods, and yet it's more than that. It sort of means garbage, dust, bastard, alien devil — it has all those connotations. It's odd—I'm sure my mom must have given me a name, but I can't remember it."

"And so that became your name, in a sense."

"Yes, it was like my identity began that day with *toogee*—garbage, bastard. That was what people called me."

"What happened next?"

"The trainmaster shooed me away, so I left and found an ox cart that was leaning up against a wall. I crawled in there the first night. I gathered some straw around me and opened the parcel and ate some food my mom had given me. I tried to sleep, but I remember hearing the dogs, the strange noises, the rustling sounds. I was scared, and yet I wasn't overly panicked."

"Even at that young age?"

"I trusted my mom, and somewhere in my mind I thought my uncle would come."

I hesitated before broaching the next question. Finally, I said, "Today, as you look back, do you think there ever really was an uncle?"

She didn't flinch. "Honestly I have no idea. It could be that she really was entrusting me to someone and I simply made a mistake by getting off at the wrong station. But in those days in Korea, it wasn't uncommon for mothers to abandon their children, especially if they were biracial. Sometimes they couldn't take the harassment, the social stigma, and being cruelly ostracized by others. They often left the children in train stations or other public areas."

"So to this day you don't really know your mother's intentions?"

Her eyes were downcast. "No, I don't," she said. Her eyes met mine again. "But I want to think the best of her. I have to, don't you see? I guess all orphans think of their mother as a princess. Still, she was under a lot of pressure, there's no question about that. Her whole future depended on it."

"I understand," I said. All of us, it seems, want to believe our parents have the best intentions. "That day at the train station started an odyssey for you. How long did it last?"

"I was basically on my own for at least two to three years. If I had stayed in the city, organizations were starting to rescue biracial children, but I was always in the mountainsides and villages."

A small child wandering aimlessly for years—what had she faced? My thoughts went to little Penelope, my cute granddaughter with the quick smile and spontaneous love for life. She's so protected, so innocent, so tenderhearted—and so dependent on her family for everything.

"I've got a granddaughter who's four years old—," I began.

"Oh, I do too!" she exclaimed.

"Then you know what I'm going to ask. You probably look at her and think, *How in the world did I survive at age four?* How *did* you manage to survive?"

"Only the Lord, I think. One thing about Third World children is that they don't have the pampering that our grandchildren do. Sometimes they don't have the degree of nurturing that our children do. Often, from the time they're little, they're sort of raising themselves. My mother had been busy in the rice fields, so she wasn't there to take care of me all the time. So that in itself was a blessing. I was already a bit self-sufficient."

Locusts and Field Mice

I imagined the bounty of food that's put before Penelope three times a day—and which, like more preschoolers, she routinely picks at with casual disinterest. "How did you manage to eat?" I asked Stephanie.

"Actually, food was plentiful in the country, except in the winter," she said. "I could steal whatever I wanted. There were fruit fields, vegetable fields, and rice fields. As long as I didn't get caught, I could eat.

"I remember following a group of homeless children. At night they would crawl on their bellies into the fields and get some of what we called sweet melons. I thought, *I could do that*. So there was a season where every night I would wait for the watchman of the field to fall asleep, and I would crawl on my belly and get what I wanted.

"Plus, the rice fields were full of grasshoppers and locusts. I would catch them and poke a rice straw through their head until I had a whole string of them, which I'd tie to my belt. By the end of the day they were pretty much dried and I'd eat them. And I killed field mice. They would come out of the same hole at the same time every day. I learned to be really, really patient. When they stuck out their head, I would grab them quicker than they could go back down the hole. I pretty much ate everything—the skin, the ears, the tail."

I asked, "What about the winters? They must have been unbearable for you."

"Yes, they were very cold, and I had nowhere to go and no food. Really, I should have died that first winter. I don't know how I survived, except I remember I found a foxhole to live in. I gathered whatever straw I could find from the rice fields and brought it in to make a little den. I'd go down to the village when everybody was sleeping and steal what I could from the villagers.

"In Third World countries, street children grow up really fast. I learned to adapt quickly. In my wanderings, everything was a treasure. A tin can thrown by a soldier from a truck became my drinking can and boiling pot. We would find nails and put them on the railroad tracks to be run over and flattened—they became utensils. I would use one to gut the mice I would catch."

"Did the villagers know you were there?"

"Oh, yes. Every once in a while a kind woman would leave her kitchen door open for me, and I would curl up on the dirt floor by the stove and stay warm. Those were answers to prayers, because in my dens I would be shivering all night."

"You mentioned earlier that you were taunted."

"It was constant. The children taunted me because I was biracial, and the farmers would yell at me because I was stealing from them. To everyone, I was a dirty *toogee*. And when you're a little child and hear people call you that day after day, you begin to believe it about yourself. I believed anyone could do whatever they wanted to me physically because I wasn't a person. I was worthless. I was dirty. I was unclean. I had no name. I had no identity. I had no family. I had no future and no hope. Over time, I began to hate myself.

"There were times when I would follow a group of homeless children. Sometimes they would let me mingle with them, and other times they would do bad things to me, you just never knew. So I became hypervigilant. Very cautious. And yet the child in me would always want to be with people. I was always looking for someone to say, 'Oh, be my friend. You can belong to us.'"

"What was it like for you emotionally?"

"I was in survival mode. I did cry when I was abused, I did beg for mercy, I would get angry, I would kick and scream, I learned cuss words really quickly. The first few days or weeks, I cried for my mommy. I was always trying to find my way back to her. Maybe she would be over the next hill; maybe she would be around the next corner. If I saw a village from the distance I would think, *Oh, that's my village*, and I would run into it.

"But it was never my village."

The Well and the Water Wheel

"You mentioned abuse," I said. "Were you victimized by people?"

"One time the farmers caught me stealing, and they threw me into some sort of abandoned cistern, like a well, hoping I would die," she replied. "I panicked, because I didn't know how to swim. There was water in the bottom, but in my thrashing I found a rock that was sticking out of the wall and I climbed up on it, though I was still sitting in some water. I remember screaming and hearing my voice echo back to me, but nobody was coming to rescue me. I honestly thought, 'Okay, I'm going to die.' And in a sense, that was okay. I thought, 'Yeah, if I just let go, I can die.'

"Finally, at dusk I heard a voice from an old woman, calling, 'Little girl, little girl, are you down there?' I hollered, 'Yes, I am.' She lowered a bucket—it was dark in there and hard to see, but I could hear the metal hitting the rocks. When it hit me, I climbed in as best as I could. She pulled me up—*clang, clang, clang, clang*, I can still hear that—and she grabbed me under my arms and dragged me to an ox stall. She covered me up with straw to get me warm, and then she brought me some food.

"Even though I had been taunted before, this was the first time it dawned on me that people might actually murder me. I thought, *Why am I so bad that people want to kill me? Why can't I be like other children who have a mommy and daddy?*"

"What did the woman say to you?"

"She told me, 'These people—they will hurt you. But it's very, very important that you must live.' As an adult looking back, I now believe those words were prophetic. But as a little girl I remember thinking that she must be telling me this because she knows my mommy. I thought she was suggesting that if I get up in the morning and I leave the village and go over the next mountaintop, my mommy will be there.

"Another time, I was also caught stealing food. I remember a farmer grabbing me by the back of my neck, calling me *toogee* and saying, 'We've got to get rid of her,' and the other farmers saying, 'Yeah, she's nothing but a menace. Let's tie her to the water wheel.'

"They grabbed me by my feet and shoulders, took me to the water wheel on the canal, and tied me face up—if I close my eyes, I can still tell you the cloud formations that I saw. I remember hearing myself scream; I remember my feet and my legs being stretched; I remember going under the water; I remember the pebbles and sand going into my mouth and nose. I remember coming up, spitting it all out, screaming, cursing. I could taste blood, my eyes got swollen — and then, all of a sudden the water wheel stopped.

"I felt a hand, and I heard a man's voice saying, 'Everything's okay. I'm going to take you off the water wheel, don't fight me.' He took me off the water wheel and placed me on the ground. My eyes were so swollen I couldn't hardly see him, but I do remember that he was wearing white. A lot of grandfathers in Korea wore white outfits back then. He took a handkerchief and cleaned me up as best as he could and gave me a drink of water.

"Then he said the same words as the woman who rescued me from the well — 'These people, they want to hurt you. You need to leave, but you must live, little girl. It's very important. Listen to me — you must live.'"

From Garbage Heap to Hope

Stephanie did continue to struggle and survive, finally wandering into Daejeon, one of the largest cities in South Korea. "This young man came toward me, called me *toogee* and said, 'You're new here in this town?' I said, 'Yes, I am.' He said, 'Do you need a place to stay?' No one had ever asked me to stay with them. I said, 'Yes, I do.' He said, 'Follow me.'

"There was a river that ran through the city, and the embankment had become a children's village. There were hundreds of orphans on both sides. He was a leader of a little gang that oversaw everything, and he let me be a part of that gang. The first few days were wonderful. When they got food, they shared with me. They had blankets that they shared with me. They built bonfires and told folk stories, and when they went to sleep I got to sleep next to this boy and other children.

"But after a few days, it became really bad. I just sort of became their plaything. I was only seven. I knew it was wrong. It wasn't just one person, it was multiple people. But in my little mind I reasoned that must happen to everybody. That's what you do to belong to a family. I just didn't realize the horror of it.

"I don't know how long I was with them, but a cholera epidemic swept through South Korea, and I became very, very sick. When you get cholera, you lose weight, you have a high fever, you become delirious. I thought, *I've got to leave here. I'll go back into the country, where the air is better and I can get fresh food. Everything will be okay.*

"I was walking through a dark alley, and I saw another child, who most likely had cholera, in an open sewage way. I went down to get her—she was screaming. I didn't know how sick we were, but I was thinking, *She's hungry, I'm hungry, so I'll go steal some food.*

"But we were caught by the farmers again. They took us to a building that had been bombed out during the war. Now, the street family had told us about this building. Where we lived along the embankments there were lots of gutter rats. They came down to the river in packs, and we were afraid of them, but as long as we were together they didn't bother us. But that building was their territory, and we were to never go in there. And the farmers—there were four or five of them—threw us in there. I can recall picking that little girl up, I remember screaming—but that's the last thing I remember."

"What's your next memory?"

"Opening my eyes and staring into blue eyes."

"Blue eyes? Whose were they?"

"I later learned her name—Iris Eriksson, a World Vision nurse from Sweden. Her job was to rescue babies from the street, because at that time children were being abandoned left and right, mainly because Korea was still trying to survive after the war, and if you had more babies than you could feed, you just abandoned them. She was told to bring back the babies—not older kids like me—because they were more likely to survive, more likely to get adopted, and less likely to have behavioral issues."

"You must have been about seven years old," I said. "So what happened to you?"

"Here's the story I was told later. She found me on a garbage heap and realized I was more sick than alive. Of course, she felt pity for me, but I was much too old for her clinic. She actually got up and was going to leave me there, but she said two things happened that changed her mind. And you need to understand Miss Eriksson was a very quiet Lutheran woman, very reserved in her faith, so this was certainly not typical for her."

"What happened?"

"As she got up and was walking away, she said her legs felt really, really heavy. She didn't know why. As she was trying to figure it out, she heard an audible voice."

I must have looked startled, because Stephanie let out a laugh. "You had to be there when she was telling it, you know? Miss Eriksson said, 'I heard a voice in my native tongue, and it only said two words: *She's mine.*' She was stunned, to say the least!"

"There was nobody around?"

"No, not a soul. She said, 'I knew it was God — and I knew I had to answer him.' So she did. She scooped me up and brought me to her clinic. She let me stay for a few weeks, and then, when I was healthy enough, she transferred me to the World Vision orphanage in the city.

"Miss Eriksson — well, how can I put this? In a way, she was my savior before Jesus."

A Man Like Goliath

The orphanage became a house, but hardly a home. The conditions were primitive — outdoor plumbing, mats for beds, and hundreds of children needing attention. "I was one of the oldest ones," Stephanie said. "My job became caring for the babies—washing the diapers, hanging up the diapers, folding the diapers, changing the children, putting them on my back while I was working. I loved the babies."

Love—that was a word I hadn't heard during the story of Stephanie's journey. "Was this a new emotion for you—building relationships with them?"

"Oh, yes. When I went into the baby section, they all had their arms out, wanting me to hold them. I felt loved. The workers didn't have enough time for all of them, so I would sing to them and hug them and carry them around. Then, every once in a while, a baby would disappear."

"Disappear?"

"Yes, and when I would ask where the baby went, they would say, 'He went to America.'"

"Oh, so they were adopted."

"Well, that's the thing—I didn't know what adoption meant. I just knew that when they said a baby went to America, it was a good thing. So one day the director said an American couple was coming to pick out a baby boy. I immediately started working to get them ready —brushing their hair, giving them a bath, pinching their cheeks, putting them in the best rags we had available.

"The next day, the bell rang in the compound. A worker opened the door, and it was like Mr. Goliath was coming in. Not only was he tall, he was massive. Back then in Korea the only people with extra weight were rich, so I thought he must be the wealthiest person on the face of the earth. He stepped aside and Mrs. Goliath came in. She wasn't much smaller.

"They were speaking English and had an interpreter with them. The bassinets were lined up along the hallway, and I watched as the man would pick up a baby and tuck it under his neck." Her face lit up at the memory.

"I was just overwhelmed by him; I don't think I had ever seen a man hold a baby like that. He brought the baby right up to his cheek, and he was kissing him and talking to him, and it was just ... well, an emotion began to rise in me. I saw him put that baby down and pick up another baby, and what I didn't realize was that I was inching closer to him. I was very curious.

"He put the second baby under his chin, and then I looked into his eyes—and he was crying. And my heart was starting to *pump pump pump pump pump*, because I knew: This is good. Something in me said, *This is good*. He put that baby down and did the same thing with a third one—and with the third one, he saw me out of the corner of his eye. He did the same, kissing and putting the baby down, and he turned around to look toward me—and I started backing up, backpedaling."

"When he looked at you, what was he seeing at that time?"

"Although I was almost nine years old and had been in the orphanage for about two years, I still had dirt on my body, especially my elbows and knees—it was ground into my skin. I had lice so bad that my head was actually white. I had worms so bad in my stomach that when they got hungry they'd crawl out of my throat. I had a lazy eye that sort of flopped around in its socket. I couldn't see very well at all, probably from malnutrition. My face was devoid of expression. I weighed a little less than thirty pounds. I was a scrawny thing. I had boils all over me and scars on my face.

"And yet still, he came over to where I was. He got down as low as he could, right down on his haunches, and looked straight into my eyes. He stretched out his enormous hand, and he laid it on my face, just like this," she said, closing her eyes as she tenderly demonstrated with her own hand. "His hand covered my head; it felt so good and so right. And then he started stroking my face."

I sat spellbound. Here it was—the image of grace I had been seeking: an aspiring father bringing unconditional acceptance to a child who had absolutely nothing to offer, no accolades or accomplishments, just herself in all of her vulnerability and scars and weaknesses.

My eyes moistened. *This* is the love of a dad. Maybe—*just maybe*—this is the love of a Father.

Slamming the Window Shut

Then something incredible happened. "The hand on my face felt so good," Stephanie was telling me, "and inside I was saying, *Oh, keep that up! Don't let your hand go!* But nobody had ever reached out to me that way before, and I didn't know how to respond."

"What did you do?"

Her eyes widened as if she were still astonished by her own actions. "I yanked his hand off my face," she said, "and I looked him in the eye—and I spit on him! Twice, I spit on him! And then I ran away and hid in a closet."

Spit on him? My mind was reeling. Grace was throwing open a window of opportunity for her—a chance for hope, security, and a future—and she deliberately slammed it shut.

"How?" I asked. "How could you possibly do that?"

Yet as she searched for a fuller explanation, my mind flooded with all the ways I had yanked God's hand off my face the many times he had reached out to me in my days of rebellion and skepticism.

There was the time as a child when a Sunday school teacher spoke glowingly about the love of God. I felt drawn toward faith—but uncomfortable with the emotions, I pulled away. Or the time at a friend's wedding when the pastor spoke powerfully about building a marriage around Christ. I was intrigued, but quickly the busyness of my career doused my budding spiritual curiosity.

Or the time I cried out to the God I didn't believe in, desperate for him to heal our newborn daughter of the mysterious illness that was threatening her life. Suddenly—somehow, inexplicably—she recovered fully, but I promptly forgot about the prayer, chalking up the healing to a miracle of modern medicine, even though the doctors had no explanation for what happened. More than once, I had to admit, I had allowed the window of spiritual opportunity to slowly ... slide ... *shut*.

For Stephanie, in many ways this could have been the end of her story. Still, incredibly, the man and woman at the orphanage were persistent. They continued to pursue her, despite her initial rejection. The next day, they came back.

"I was called into the director's office, and there was the foreign couple," Stephanie was telling me. "I was thinking, *I'm in real trouble now! I'm going to get punished for what I did to him. They're going to beat the tar out of me.* But the interpreter pointed to this man and this woman—these strangers, these foreigners, this enormous man with the huge heart who wept over children—and she said, 'They want to take you to their house.'"

What struck me was that this couple could easily have chosen a more compliant child—perhaps the baby boy they had originally envisioned adopting, a child without the emotional baggage and physical ailments of this recalcitrant street girl, someone who was not suffering from the effects of years of deprivation and abuse, someone who wouldn't require as much of a sacrifice to parent. Nobody would have blamed them. Nobody would have given it a second thought. Nevertheless, David and Judy Merwin, newly arrived missionaries from the United States, unexpectedly declared on that day: *This is the child we want.*

"At the time, I didn't realize that I was being adopted," Stephanie said. "I thought I was going to become their servant. That's basically what happened in Korea: when a child got a certain age, he or she was sold as a bond servant to rich people."

A servant—yes, she could envision that. She could pay off their kindness, she could work her way out of her indebtedness, she could repay them for taking a risk on her, she could earn her room and board. Becoming a servant was the only way she could make any sense of her situation. A very understandable reaction.

"There Are No Words"

The Merwins had expected to adopt a boy and name him Stephen, so they gave their new little girl the name Stephanie. Their house in Korea, modest by Western standards, seemed huge to her.

"I had never seen a refrigerator, a flush toilet, or a bed before. I thought, *Wow, this will be a fun place to work!* They even had eggs, which only affluent Koreans could afford. They cleaned me up, gave me antibiotics, and got me healthy. They kept feeding me, tucking me into bed, buying me new clothes, but never putting me to work."

"Did that confuse you?"

"Yes, I wondered why for several months, but I was afraid to bring it up to them. We'd go into a village, and everybody would treat me like I was something wonderful. I couldn't understand — I had been a *toogee*, but now I was being treated like a princess.

"Then one day a girl said to me, 'You smell American.' I said, 'What do you mean?' She said, 'You smell like cheese.' Korean children always said foreigners smelled like cheese. I said, 'No, I'm not an American, but those Americans are really funny. They haven't put me to work yet. They're really treating me nice.'

"She looked at me with a surprised expression and said, 'Stephanie, don't you realize that you're their daughter?' That idea had never occurred to me. I said, 'No, I'm not their daughter!' And she said, 'Yes, you are! *You ... are ... their ... daughter.*'

"I was astonished! I turned and ran out of the room and up the hill toward my house, thinking to myself, *I'm their daughter, I'm their daughter, I'm their daughter! Oh, that's why I've been treated this way.*

That's why no one's beating me. That's why nobody's calling me a toogee. *I'm their daughter!*

"I ran into the house to my mom, who was sitting in a chair, and I declared in Korean, 'I'm your daughter!' She didn't speak Korean yet, but a worker said to my mom, 'She's saying she's your daughter.' With that, big tears began to run down my mommy's face. She nodded and said to me, 'Yes, Stephanie, you're my daughter!' "

"How did that make you feel?"

Stephanie had been speaking so candidly about her life, including unthinkable mistreatment and suffering, abandonment and rejection, humiliation and pain. But now she was flustered. This time, words failed her.

"It was — ," she began, then threw up her hands. "There are no words, Lee. There are simply no words."

Sometimes language cannot contain grace.

And Then, Jesus

"Your adoptive parents showed you so much love," I said. "Did that point you toward Jesus? How did you end up becoming a Christian?"

"We were at a beach in Korea, and my daddy asked me if I wanted to be baptized, and I said, 'Sure, let's just do it in the ocean.' So my daddy baptized me."

"Did you really have faith at that point, or were you trying to please your parents?"

"I loved the Lord as much as I knew how, but I just had so much hurt inside. My problem was that I was scared to show people my pain. If my mommy and daddy saw my pain, I thought they would bring me back to the orphanage. If my teachers saw my pain, they would tell my parents. If my friends saw my pain, they'd tell my parents. I never wanted them to find out about my life as a street kid. I was afraid they'd reject me. That went on until I was about seventeen."

"What happened then?"

"We had moved to a small town in Indiana, where my father was a pastor, and I was doing everything to deny my Korean heritage. I was the only Asian in high school, and I wanted to be the perfect American girl. I was the homecoming queen and won the citizenship award, yet every night I'd go to bed scared to death I'd be discovered and lose my parents' love.

"Then the summer before my seventeenth birthday, I was sullen and irritable and withdrawn, and my mom gently confronted me. I stalked off to my bedroom, shut the door, and looked in the mirror. I felt like I was still nothing but a *toogee*, a piece of trash. I crawled under the covers of my bed.

"A little while later, my dad opened the door, and I heard him call softly, 'Stephanie?' He came in and sat next to my bed and said, 'Your mother and I want you to know that we love you very much, but you seem to have a hard time accepting that love. The time has come for us to release you to God.'

"Now, I was a pastor's daughter, so I knew the Bible, right? But my dad knew better. He said, 'Stephanie, can I share with you about Jesus?' I sort of rolled my eyes and said, 'Sure.' He told me to think about Jesus—he knows how I feel, and he is the only one who can help me. And then my daddy left me by myself.

"Until that moment, I only saw Jesus as the Son of God. I knew he had come down to earth, but that night for the first time it dawned on me: *He understands me.* He walked in my shoes! As a matter of fact, he was sort of a *toogee*. You know? His daddy—his earthly father—wasn't his real daddy. He slept in the straw as a child. He was ridiculed and abused. They chased him and tried to kill him.

"And it was dawning on me, *Oh, that's what daddy means when he says Jesus understands me.* So after my dad left that night, I prayed—but my prayer was not a nice prayer. I said 'God, if you're what

mom and dad say you are, then do something and do it right now!'
And he did."

"What did he do?"

"I started crying. I hadn't cried in years; I hadn't been able to. In
the process of being abused and taunted, I realized that the more I
cried, the more pain I would experience. But that night something
cold and hard broke inside of me — a barrier between me and God.
He finally let me shed tears — and I couldn't stop them.

"I started wailing, and my mom and dad came into the room.
They didn't say anything. I wouldn't let them snuggle with me, so my
dad held my feet and my mom held my hands and they prayed silently
to the Lord. And I had this supernatural intervention.

"Suddenly, it just came to me: Jesus knows me — *and he still loves
me!* He knows all my shame, he knows all my guilt, he knows all my
fears, he knows all my loneliness — yet he still loves me. And I've never
been the same since.

"Before then, when I would hear about God's love, I always felt
it was love for everyone else. He couldn't love me, right? I was a mistake! He couldn't love me — I was born out of sin. He couldn't love
me — I'm biracial. I thought you had to have some status in life to be
loved. That was so ingrained in me that after I was adopted and my
parents talked about the love of God, I still thought, *He can't love me!
I was raped. He can't love me! I was abused. He can't love me! I have this
awful anger inside. He can't love me! My daddy says I need to forgive, and
I just don't want to.*

"But that night came the realization: *He ... loves ... me!* He loves
me as I am. And that changed me, inside out. It took me many, many
more years to let go of certain patterns in my life and to heal. I hated
myself for so long. The fact that I could finally look in the mirror and
love myself was nothing less than a miracle. It's God's grace.

"So these days I have a phrase that I use. For me, I can honestly say there is no event in my life that I am better without. Why? Because everything in my life brought me to Jesus."

"That's radical, Stephanie, given all you've been through."

"Maybe so, but that's what I live on. I counsel a lot of women with abuse in their past—in fact, that's a large part of my ministry today—and they're always looking for a finished resolution. Maybe that will happen for some of them—I hope so. But for me, that's not going to happen until heaven."

"And when you get there," I said, "what do you want to ask Jesus?"

Stephanie settled back in her chair. She glanced out the window, where the afternoon sunshine had chased away the Oregon gray, and then she looked back at me.

"You know," she said, her smile gentle, "some people say they will ask tons of questions when they get to the other side. And that's fine. But I don't think that way anymore. I've come to realize that when I get to the other side, then I won't need the answers."

I nodded. "I think I understand," I said. "But your story is so completely different from mine that I can't imagine how you're able to process it all."

She took a sip from a cup of coffee on the table next to her. "Maybe we have more in common than you think," she said.

I wasn't sure what she meant. In an earlier conversation, in response to her questions about my background, I had mentioned the issues that prompted my exploration of grace, but I still didn't see the connection she was referring to.

"The Bible talks about orphans, but sometimes it uses the word *fatherless*," she said. "It sounds like your father protected and provided for you—believe me, that's good. You should be grateful for that, as I'm sure you are. But still, a person can be an orphan of the heart."

An orphan of the heart. I shuddered. Her words penetrated to my core.

"And that's where God can provide," she said. "That's where grace can come in. As the psalm says, 'Thou, God, art the helper of the fatherless.' "[3]

Adopted by God

As I flew back to Denver the next day, I felt as if I'd looked into the eyes of grace. Once untrusting, uncertain, and anticipating the worst, today Stephanie's gaze is warm, gentle, and serenely confident. Such a remarkable transformation, first because of a father who sacrificed his dream of a son and reached out to her when she was a social untouchable, and then because of a Father who sacrificed his own Son in order to lavish on her a redemptive and healing love.

Now she spends her life counseling broken young women, sharing with them her story, and capping it with the most unlikely of declarations: *I can honestly say there is no event in my life that I am better without.*

Over the telephone, I related the details of our conversation to my longtime friend Mark Mittelberg, and a few days later we met for lunch in a dusty café on the Front Range of Colorado.

"Do you remember this?" Mark asked, tossing a dog-eared paperback on the table.

I picked it up and smiled. It was a forty-year-old edition of theologian J. I. Packer's classic book *Knowing God*, a volume of insights that I had researched during my initial investigation of Christianity and which has sat on my shelf for decades.

"Sure, I remember it," I said as I paged through his copy, which had sentences emphatically underlined and stars penciled in the margins. "I mean, I remember that it clarified a lot of issues for me, but I can't recall many of the specifics. Why did you bring it?"

"Because of what you told me about Stephanie," he said. "Don't you remember? One of Packer's big points is that you can't fully appreciate grace apart from adoption. Here—listen to this," he said, grabbing back the book, flipping to a page and reading: " 'If you want to judge how well a person understands Christianity, find out how much he makes of the thought of being God's child, and having God as his Father. If this is not the thought that prompts and controls his worship and prayers, and his whole outlook on life, it means that he does not understand Christianity very well at all.' "[4]

He put down the book. "Don't you see? Your life has been a quest for grace, and you've seen a unique picture of it in Stephanie. Twice she has been adopted, both times ambushed by grace. That's what has resonated with you—her story of finding the ultimate love of a perfect Father."

He was right—and *that's* when it crystalized for me. What truly captivates me about grace is that God has not only erased the sins for which I deserved punishment, but he has become my loving and compassionate Father, whose divine acceptance of me rushes in to fill a heart left parched by an earthly dad.

The truth is that God could have forgiven my past and given me assurance of heaven and yet kept me at arm's length. He could have made me a mere servant in his kingdom household—and even that would have been more than I merited. But his grace is far more outrageous than that.

"To be right with God the judge is a great thing," writes Packer, "but to be loved and cared for by God the father is greater."[5]

Of course, I've understood the theology behind adoption for a long time. After nearly two years of satisfying myself intellectually that Christianity was true, the last verse I read before surrendering my life to Jesus was John 1:12: "Yet to all who did receive him, to those who believed in his name, he gave the right to become children of God."

Children of God—yes, I have long understood that God's grace invites us into his eternal family. But this was the day, sitting in that café, when the grace of adoption struck me afresh and registered deep inside of me. The puzzle pieces fit together more snugly than ever.

"It is like a fairy story," wrote Packer. "The reigning monarch adopts waifs and strays to make princes of them—but, praise God, it is not a fairy story: it is hard and solid fact, founded on the bedrock of free and sovereign grace. This, and nothing less than this, is what adoption means. No wonder that John cries, 'Behold, what manner of love ...!' When you understand adoption, your heart will cry the same."[6]

My mind reveled in the image of Stephanie, running with unrestrained joy toward home, declaring to herself, *I'm their daughter, I'm their daughter, I'm their daughter! Oh, that's why I've been treated this way. That's why no one's beating me. That's why nobody's calling me a toogee. I'm their daughter!*

I desperately needed to absorb this truth anew: I'm beyond forgiven. I'm more than a servant. I'm adopted by a Father whose love is perfect, whose acceptance is unconditional, whose affection is neverending, and whose generosity is boundless. A Father who is *for* me ... forever.

As much as I tried to temper it in the midst of the crowded café, a broad smile spread over my face. I couldn't mask the celebration that was breaking out inside of me. Once again, I found myself running toward Home.

I'm his son, I'm his son, I'm his son! Oh, that's why I've been treated this way. I'm his son!

CHAPTER 3

The Addict

We Can Escape to the Freedom of Grace

Grace is wild. Grace unsettles everything. Grace overflows the banks. Grace messes up your hair. Grace is not tame.... Unless we are making the devout nervous, we are not preaching grace as we ought.

Doug Wilson[1]

H is heart racing, his body soaked in sweat, his mind dazed and disoriented, the teenager slowly regained consciousness. He wasn't sure where he was. It took every ounce of his energy just to crawl out of the bed. There in the mirror he barely recognized himself—gaunt, sunken eyes, detached expression. After the cocktail of drugs he had consumed, he was a little surprised that he was still alive.

That's when he proceeded to do something that only another addict could fathom: he mixed his remaining stash of drugs, drew a breath—and plunged the needle into his arm once again.

I might die, he mused. *And I'm okay with that.*

If anyone needed God's help, it was this seventeen-year-old Texan. After four years of descending into a hell of cocaine and methamphetamines, he was rushing headlong toward an early death.

So what becomes of a budding auto thief, a shoplifter, a slacker, a drug abuser who started injecting meth before he was old enough to drive? Well, there I was, sitting with him in his office inside a megachurch located in—of all places—Las Vegas, the mecca of vice.

Yes, now he's the pastor of a church. And because of his experiences, he has a generous attitude toward this metropolis nicknamed Sin City. His office wall is dominated by a large photograph of the Las Vegas Strip, awash in the purples and oranges of sunset. Emblazed across the top in bold letters are the words "Grace City." Along the bottom is Romans 5:20: "Where sin increased, grace increased all the more."

Sin and grace—I knew those themes were central to Jud Wilhite's story, but during our years of friendship he had never shared with me the details of his rescue from the edge of a drug-induced death. I was anxious to hear what happened, but I traveled to Las Vegas for more than that, because there's another dimension to Jud's journey that especially intrigued me.

It involves what happened *after* Jud was adopted by grace into God's family. Soon he found that he had traded one addiction for another compulsion. This time, it was performance and legalism that threatened to suffocate his faith—just as it had mine.

As it turns out, we both came to the place where we desperately needed a fresh breath of God's grace.[2]

Ensnared by Drugs

When Jud was twelve, he joined a cluster of students passing around a joint during a lunch break outside his junior high school. That was when he was introduced to drugs.

"It wasn't so much about getting high," he recalled. "It was more about my self-esteem and my desire to fit in with the kids who were older than me."

Even today, Jud looks younger than his forty-two years. His black-rimmed glasses, slightly spikey hair, and dark clothing give him a hipster look; one visiting journalist said he dressed like a roadie for a rock band. He has been married to Lori for more than seventeen years, and they have a son and a daughter, who is now almost the same age as Jud when he first smoked pot.

"All addicts tell the same story," Jud said to me. "When it starts out, you go to parties and the drugs make you feel good, like you're freer and can communicate better. But in short order, you don't even go to the party anymore, because you're in a back room somewhere, doing the heaviest stuff you can find. You're on the path to jail, death, or insanity — one of those three. Unless you get clean, it's going to happen. And it didn't take me long to find my way to that back room."

Drugs were readily available in Amarillo, where Jud grew up as a fourth child, with a big gap between him and the next oldest sibling — just like me. His dad was a former Army master sergeant who had fought at the Battle of the Bulge, later finding success in owning a refrigeration business.

"Did your parents take you to church as a kid?" I asked.

"Yeah," he said, "I'd tell them I was going to the youth group, then I'd sneak out the back and walk around the alley, smoking cigarettes and waiting for church to be over. I'd meet them at the car afterward."

"Did they ever ask you about the youth group?"

"Oh, sure. They'd say, 'What did you learn about today?' I'd say, 'Jesus.' They'd say, 'What about him?' And I'd say, 'That he loves me.' I figured that was what they wanted to hear."

Pot and booze led to speed and cocaine. His life tumbled out of control. Police arrested him after he was caught shoplifting at a department store. When he was fourteen, he and some friends stole a neighbor's car late one night and took it on a joyride, with Jud behind the wheel — until they were busted by his dad.

For four years after he took his first drag of pot, everything was a blur. "I didn't know what it was like to face a week of life sober," he said.

He gestured at a guitar mounted on his wall, a memento from his days in a rock band. "It was like Johnny Cash said. After the first pill, every one he took was trying to recapture that first high — and it did nothing but drive him farther from God and the people he loved the most. That was me."

"I Can't Do This Alone"

After waking up from his overdose and then ingesting the remainder of his drugs — "I was daring death, in a way" — Jud drifted in and out of consciousness, at times vomiting violently as he clutched the bumper of his car, finally finding himself immobilized by exhaustion, lying on the floor of his darkened bedroom.

He had hit bottom, and for the first time in years, he wanted to be free — from drugs, from despair, from confusion.

"I was just a fool," he told me. "I had been given every opportunity. I had a family that loved me. But I was completely deceived by sin. I looked around and realized that my life was a train wreck."

Over the next few weeks, as he continued to smoke pot — "which was as natural to me as breathing" — Jud contemplated his future. He was at a crossroads.

"I was on the edge of everything coming unraveled," he said. "I was so tired and worn out. I hated everything I had been doing. I hated the drugs, like so many addicts do. I felt like my time was running out. If I kept on the road I was on, sooner or later I'd hit a dead end. For the first time, I realized that I was powerless to end the cycle of despair and guilt."

"So what did you do?"

"The only thing I *could* do — I cried out to God. I dropped to my knees in my bedroom and said: *God, help me! I'm messed up beyond belief. I need you!* It wasn't eloquent, but what else could I say? It was the truth."

"Then what happened?"

"Well, I didn't hear any voices or see any angels. But honestly, the sense I had in my soul was, *Welcome home.* I felt like I'd arrived at the place where I belonged."

"And that was the beginning of your turnaround?"

"Absolutely. The next morning I had my drug paraphernalia laid out in my car, and I was going sixty or seventy miles an hour down the freeway. I thought, *This is real now. What am I going to do?* I felt God giving me the courage to gather up all that stuff and throw it out the window. And that was it. I never went back."

"Did you go through withdrawal?"

"For days I was sweaty, clammy, cranky, irritable—yeah," he replied, "but I knew two things: I couldn't go back—that was simply not an option—and yet I couldn't go forward by myself. I needed a power that went beyond my own weak will. Every day I had to fight my desire for another high. It was a struggle; for a long time it was tough."

"How did you manage to break through?"

"Over and over, I kept whispering a prayer: *I can't do this alone. God, help me. If you don't show up somewhere in my life, I'm through.*"

"And did he show up?"

Jud smiled, then let out a chuckle. "Yeah, he did, but not in the way I ever expected."

"How?" I asked.

"Through the church."

Rescued by Grace

Jud Wilhite was accustomed to walking through Hillside Christian Church on his way to loitering in the alley while his parents attended services. But for the first time, at age seventeen, he walked across the parking lot and into the sanctuary on his own terms. He wasn't there because he fully believed the Christian story—not yet, anyway. He just knew his life had been a mess and he couldn't conquer his addiction on his own.

He found his way to a back room where some young people gathered each week for a Bible study. Through this small community of Christians he found Jesus.

"In some ways, they were the oddballs—the people who didn't fit in with the regular youth group," he said, "and frankly, that's what I was. A couple of them knew about my addiction, but most didn't. It didn't matter, though. They knew without knowing—you know what I mean? And they gave me a safe place."

"They showed you grace."

"Exactly. They didn't judge or condemn me. They didn't ask too many questions about my past or what I'd been involved in. They didn't sit me down like a tribunal and interrogate me. They gave me the freedom to tell them what I was comfortable telling them. They listened to me, they respected me, they prayed for me—really, they talked me off the ledge. They gave me the gift of time. They loved me like Jesus would."

Jud Wilhite had discovered the church.

Over the next six months, his appetite for God became insatiable. He would come home from school, lock himself in his room, and read the Bible cover to cover. He would hang out with members of the church group during the week. By January of his senior year, that prayer of desperation he had blurted out in his bedroom had finally been cemented. He was fully, safely, securely Home.

More and more, the church became like a family to him. One day he was strolling down the hallway when he encountered the senior pastor walking in the opposite direction.

"Hey, Jud," he said, "have you ever thought of becoming a pastor?" Just like that—out of nowhere.

Jud's first thought: *What's he been smoking?*

Still, a seed had been planted. When the two of them met later, the pastor told Jud that God had impressed on him that someday Jud would lead a church.

"How did you respond to that?" I asked.

"I prayed for two things. First, that God would let me use my experiences to help other people find the same kind of grace that had rescued me. And second, that he would allow me to do that through a local church, because God used the church to save my life."

At the time, Jud didn't foresee the biggest obstacle in his path. Religion.

Resigning from the Faith

Fueled by gratitude for God's grace, Jud shifted into high gear as a Christian. He attended a Christian camp, met some musicians, and then played bass for a Christian rock band. ("What was the band called?" "Please, don't ask." "No, seriously—what was its name?" Pause. "Angelic Force." Awkward pause. "Okay, sorry I asked.")

Later he went to a Christian college in preparation for becoming a pastor. By his senior year he attended classes during the week, then preached at a small church outside of Dallas on Sundays. But somewhere along the way, the sincere desire to serve God morphed into the compulsion to prove over and over that he was good enough to deserve God's continuing love.

"For a long time, I had failed my family and God. So after I became a Christian, I got on a performance treadmill without realizing it," he explained. "I was putting pressure on myself to please God, as if I had to maintain my good standing with him by being a super Christian. I wanted to make up for lost time and show that God was justified in saving me."

"What would you do?"

"I fasted for days. I prayed endlessly. I served the homeless. I gave away everything I owned until all I had was a pair of jeans, a shirt,

and shoes. People would talk about how mature I was as a Christian
— and, yeah, I was doing some good things, but it was for the wrong
motivation. And I wanted others to be as sacrificial as I was. When
they weren't, I was critical of them. I became a judgmental jerk."

"Sounds like you were missing the real implications of grace."

"Yeah. I knew that I was saved by God's grace alone, but now I was
trying to earn my keep. Jesus had paid my debt, but I felt like I needed
to repay him. Still, no matter how much I'd serve, pray, or sacrifice,
it was never enough. In my mind, I kept falling short. I started to feel
phony, like I was only as good as my last performance — and my last
performance wasn't very good."

I was nodding as he spoke because I could relate to his story. After
God's grace unshackled me from my atheism, I was full of boundless
energy to serve Jesus and tell others about him. I left my journalism
career and took a sixty percent cut in pay to join the staff of a church,
where I was thrilled to spend the best hours of my day in ministry.

Like Jud, I knew that I had been adopted as a child of God through
his freely offered grace, but pretty soon I found myself toiling fever-
ishly to somehow show that he had made the right choice. I needed
to demonstrate through my ministry that I was good enough for God
after all. As odd as it sounds, I was working overtime at the church to
justify the redemption that I could never have earned in the first place.

One night I got a call from the church's senior pastor, Bill Hybels.
"I heard a nasty rumor about you," he said.

I was taken aback. "Like what?"

"That you're working at the church sixty or seventy hours a week.
That you're there late into the night and all day Sunday."

To be honest, I swelled with pride. *That's right,* I wanted to say.
*I'm the hardest working member of the staff. Finally, it's time for some
recognition and thanks — if not directly from God, then from my pastor.*

I said with some modesty: "Well, I am working hard, if that's what
you mean."

Now his voice had an edge. "If you continue down that path, you're fired."

"What?"

"Something unhealthy is driving you. There's nothing you can do that will cause God to love you any more than he already does. You need to relax in that fact. Otherwise, I'm not going to be a party to your self-destruction."

I told Jud my story, and now he was the one nodding. "That's the performance trap that ensnares so many Christians," he said. "It's the rigidity of religion—following all the rules perfectly to keep God happy and condemning others because they aren't trying as hard as you. I got to the point where I was exhausted, frustrated, and miserable."

"So what did you do?"

Jud threw his hands up. "I quit!"

"You quit? How?"

"One day I said, *God, I'm not good enough. I wasn't really a church guy before anyway. I'm a former addict, for goodness' sake. I can't do this Christian thing. I quit!*"

Jumping Off the Treadmill

Jud was describing an epidemic in Christianity.[3] "We are saved by grace, but we are living by the 'sweat' of our own performance," observed author Jerry Bridges.[4] Many Christians, said Walter Marshall, are addicted to salvation by works and "find it hard to believe that you should get any blessing before you work for it."[5] Ken Blue blamed his bleeding ulcers, troubled marriage, and depression on years of jumping through religious hoops so God would give him a passing grade as a pastor.[6]

Some, like Jud, simply decide to drop out, exhausted and exasperated. "I figured I'd change my major at college and pursue some other career," Jud said. "I told God, *I still love you, but please don't ask any more of me.*"

I considered what would have happened if Jud had continued on that detour. What would have become of the church where we were sitting—a citadel of hope and grace, whose address, appropriately enough, is on New Beginnings Drive?

"What changed your mind?" I asked.

"One day I was reading 1 John 4:10, which says, 'This is love: not that we loved God, but that he loved us and sent his Son as an atoning sacrifice for our sins.' That's when it registered for me: *It's all about God.* How I feel about God isn't as important as how God feels about me. It doesn't matter how good I try to be; what's important is how good God is. He never demanded that I become a super Christian in the first place; all he asked was that I love him in return. That was transformative for me."

"It all comes back to grace."

"That's right. All we needed when we first came to Jesus was his grace, and grace is all we need to grow in Christ. Grace liberates us. Our tendency toward performance imprisons us."

"That's the message of Galatians," I suggested.

"Yes, Paul was warning the Galatians about false teachers, who were preaching that in addition to faith in Christ they needed to live according to religious rules and regulations. Paul had stopped trying to meet those requirements so that he could live for God.[7] The law was always intended to lead us beyond ourselves to the one who gives us life by grace.

"Trying to live by rules had spiritually sapped the Galatians. Paul asked them, 'What has happened to all your joy?'[8] He said they were foolish because 'after beginning by means of the Spirit,' they were 'now trying to finish by means of the flesh.'[9] It's God's grace that leads to freedom—Paul said, 'Do not let yourselves be burdened again by a yoke of slavery.' "[10]

Jud was right. It's not by accident that Paul opens and closes his letter to the Galatians by using the word *grace*.[11]

The insights that freed Jud were similar to the ones that led to my own recovery from spiritual workaholism after being confronted by my boss years ago. I came to realize that God didn't love me because I made myself valuable through service; on the contrary, I was valuable because I was loved by God. I could stop working like a slave to justify myself; I just needed to recognize — and celebrate — my adoption as God's child. My desire to love and serve God in a healthy way would flow from that.

"So how did the Bible's teachings change you?" I asked Jud.

"After I rediscovered the beauty of grace, I began to relax in my faith. I started to enjoy God again instead of feeling like I had to prove something to him. Like where Jesus said, 'Come to me, all you who are weary and burdened, and I will give you rest.'[12] The word *rest*, in Greek, means 'revive,' or 'restore.' God offers to revive us from the inside out — and that's what he did for me.

"I felt like I was free to laugh, to be myself, and to mess up. I stopped policing others and started loving them. I was freed to be compassionate toward hurting people who don't have their lives together or who might have lifestyles different from mine. I stopped putting a lot of pressure on myself. I'm not perfect — I sin every day, but I've lowered my expectations of myself and others, while I've raised my expectations of God and his grace."

"As a pastor, has it changed the way you preach?"

"Pastors have to be careful. We encourage people to serve, to give, to be part of a small group, to read their Bibles, and so forth — all of which are fine as long as they're done out of gratitude to God. But if we subtly convey that this is how someone stays on God's good side, then we're opening the door to legalism.

"I've been there," he added. "And I'm not going back."

Erring on the Side of Grace

In the early 1900s, liquor flowed and gambling flourished in the saloons of Block 16, a scrap of Las Vegas on First Street between Ogden and Stewart Avenues. Brothels thrived upstairs and in back rooms, servicing travelers and rail-yard workers. It was here that the nickname "Sin City" was coined. Today, the location has been paved over as parking lots, but the reputation of Las Vegas persists.[13]

"Our nickname came from sinners—drunkards, addicts, gamblers, failures, prostitutes, swindlers," said Jud. "In other words, people God loves."

Ever since Jud stumbled into the small community of grace-filled Christians in the back room of Hillside Christian Church in Amarillo, he has been trying to reproduce the qualities he found there. As leader of Central Christian Church, he creates a safe place where spiritually wandering people can progress at their own pace toward the same grace that saved him from addiction and despair.

His enthusiasm is uncorked when he describes the divine action at his church. "We're like a MASH unit. We're on the frontlines as a spiritual hospital," he said, inching to the edge of the couch. "I mean, bullets are flying! These people are hurting, and we've got to help them. At times, it's triage.

"What's different about Vegas is that I rarely have to convince people that sin exists. They believe in darkness; they've seen it. Some people aren't sure there's a God, but they believe in the Devil. A lot of people deal with so much guilt, shame, and brokenness that it can take years for them to allow God's grace to sink in."

"How do you avoid making them feel judged so you can give them space to grow toward God?" I asked.

"I try—imperfectly—to follow the example of Jesus. The Bible says he 'welcomes sinners and eats with them.'[14] Now, think about that. In his culture, to dine with someone meant to offer friendship.

The word *welcome* in Greek means that he took great pleasure in them. Jesus doesn't delight in sin, but he liked being around these people, maybe because they were well aware of their depravity, unlike many of the religious folks who masked it with hypocrisy.

"Think about the Samaritan woman who Jesus encountered at the well.[15] Of all the people in the world God could have made an appointment with—the politicians, the celebrities, the military conquerors—he decides to meet with a woman who's not a complete ethnic Jew and who's a five-time divorcée who was currently living with a guy," Jud said with a quick laugh.

"Jesus says to her, 'Give me a drink.' Offering a drink in those days was an act of friendship," Jud said. "You can loosely paraphrase Jesus's statement as, 'Will you be my friend?' To me, this says God loves broken people—and he loves to fix them. Look at her: she was transformed. So when I deal with people, I want to have Jesus's attitude, which is why I try to err on the side of grace."

"What do you mean by that?"

"None of us knows the motivation in the heart of another person. We can easily misread them based on how they look or dress. So if I'm likely to be wrong on my initial assessment anyway, why not give people the benefit of the doubt? If I have a choice of being harsh or gracious, I choose to be gracious—because that's the way Jesus has been with me."

"Sort of like the saying, 'Hate the sin, love the sinner,'" I said. "Do you think that's really possible?"

"Unfortunately, a lot of Christians hate the sin *and* the sinner, and it has given churches a bad reputation. But C. S. Lewis made the point that we hate sin but love the sinner all the time—in our own lives. In other words, when we're judging ourselves, we always love the sinner despite our sin. We accept ourselves, even though we might not always like our behavior."

Later I looked up Lewis' words, which came in his classic book

Mere Christianity. "However much I might dislike my own cowardice or conceit or greed, I went on loving myself," Lewis wrote. "There had never been the slightest difficulty about it."[16]

Grace and Truth

When I was a spiritual seeker investigating whether Christianity made sense, I needed time on my journey to Jesus. Nearly two years elapsed between the moment I walked into a church in suburban Chicago and when I received Jesus as my forgiver and leader. Along the way, I also needed to be confronted periodically by the Bible's hard teachings on sin, confession, repentance, judgment—and, yes, even on hell.

"Jesus modeled grace, but he also embodied truth," I said to Jud. "The Bible says the law was given through Moses, but grace and truth came through Christ.[17] Are you shying away from the more challenging truths of the Bible in order to keep people coming back to your church?"

Jud's smile was good-natured. "I'm open to using any legitimate methodology to reach people with the gospel, but theologically I'm conservative," he said. "Sometimes when critics see a large church, they scoff and say, 'If they were preaching the truth, they wouldn't be attracting big crowds.' But that's not accurate."

He sat back and crossed his legs. "I find guidance in the letters that Paul wrote to the Corinthian church because there are similarities between ancient Corinth and modern Vegas."

"Like what?"

"Corinth was the Sin City of its day, sort of a tourist mecca. It was so identified with sexual immorality that Plato once referred to a prostitute as a 'Corinthian girl.'[18] Aristophanes even used the city's name in creating a Greek verb that meant 'to fornicate.'[19] The Corinthian church was filled with people who were on spiritual journeys but hadn't arrived yet. There was strife and arguments and immorality going on — it was a mess. So what did Paul do? How did he reach out to them?

"First, he emphasized grace; in fact, he mentions grace twice in the opening verses of First Corinthians.[20] And in a gracious but specific and pointed way, he goes on to confront and teach them on everything from sexual behavior to lawsuits to marriage.

"Then, second, he anchors everything in truth — specifically, in the reality of the resurrection of Jesus. He says if Jesus didn't really rise from the dead in an actual event of history, then our faith is worthless and we're hopelessly mired in our sin.[21]

"I see grace and truth as two sides of the same coin. If Christianity isn't true — actually, literally, really true — then grace is meaningless. It's just an empty promise or wishful thinking. All that's left would be what theologian Richard Niebuhr called 'a God without wrath who brought men without sin into a kingdom without judgment through the ministrations of a Christ without a cross.' "[22]

"So you preach in the sex capital of America on what the Bible teaches about sexual morality?"

He chuckled. "Just this last weekend, I did a message on sexual purity. I told the congregation, 'Look, if you're dealing with sexual sin in your life, you need to run from it — but don't run away from God.' I didn't water down what the Bible teaches, but I also allowed room for people to process it. I said, 'If you're just starting a spiritual journey, you need to know that God loves you even in the midst of your sin.'

"Now, that offends some critics, who think you need to browbeat everybody to prove to the world that you're legit and that you stand up for truth. Instead, I want to spell out biblical truth in a way that's accurate but also gracious and encouraging.

"You see, we want people to go on a journey, but we don't want them to just wander around aimlessly, without direction. We want to guide them with God's Word. For us, there's always a destination in mind—and that's the cross. That's where we want to see them end up—receiving forgiveness and hope through Jesus's atoning death."

Addicted to Grace

Jud glanced at the poster of the nighttime Las Vegas Strip under the words "Grace City." He gathered his thoughts and then offered a story about a woman who had been attending his church for a while.

"I'll call her Sadie," he said. "She was a dancer in the adult entertainment world, which is pretty much a euphemism for being a stripper. Something started to draw her to our church. She would dance all night, finishing in the early morning hours on Sunday, and then come over for the early service.

"At first, she sat in the farthest reaches of the balcony. Over time she worked her way closer to the platform, until eventually she was sitting in the front row. She soaked in everything. She heard about grace and truth. She examined her life. She felt the Spirit working in her. She counted the cost. Then one Sunday she came up to me after a service and said she wanted to become a Christian.

"She told me her whole unvarnished story. When she finished, I said, 'If you make this decision to follow Jesus, what will it mean for you?' And she didn't flinch. She said, 'It's going to affect my career, it's going to affect my income, it's going to change my whole life.' I said, 'Well, what are you waiting for?' And her voice was firm; she said: 'I'm ready.'

"So she began to pray—not a tidy fill-in-the-blank kind of prayer, but a raw confession, followed by sincere repentance and sort of a delightful childlike acceptance of God's gift of grace.

"When she said, 'Amen,' we opened our eyes. Her mascara was a mess; there were tears spilling down her cheeks. She reached out to give me a hug, and all she could say was, 'Thank you, thank you, thank you!'"

Jud beamed as he recalled the encounter. He was quiet for a moment, like he didn't know what to say to me next. Finally came this: "I remember when I was a young pastor at a little church when I was in graduate school, and I had to scrub out the baptistery because it hadn't been used for so long.

"Here in Vegas, we baptized nearly two thousand people last year. Every one of them — like Sadie — has a story. And mostly, they're messy — sometimes *really* messy. But every single story matters to God."

He grinned. "I guess, in a way, I'm still an addict," he said. "I can't get enough of that."

CHAPTER 4

The Professor

God's Grace Is Like Nothing Else in the World

*I'm holding out for grace. I'm holding out that Jesus took
my sins onto the cross, because I know who I am, and I
hope I don't have to depend on my own religiosity.*

Bono[1]

Craig Hazen has always been the good guy. Smart, well-mannered, witty, his spirit gentle and his grin easy, he was a teacher's favorite in high school because — in a rarity among teenagers — he actually *liked* to learn. When he walked into the library, he felt like he was on a treasure hunt.

Hazen was a science geek before the term was invented, working after school as an assistant to a physician and planning a career in medical research. Sure, he was mischievous, once instigating an enormous donut fight that became enshrined in school lore, but he was clever enough to get away with it. The honor roll — that was no problem. He was enthralled with the process of discovery.

As for nice guys, they don't need God. At least, that was Hazen's opinion. As a teenager, he became an agnostic, figuring that science — not theology — held the keys to understanding the big issues of life.

Still, there was that chemistry teacher, the one who kept putting cryptic posters about God on her classroom walls — she had an undeniable sense of peace that intrigued him. And then there was the cute girl who invited him to church one night to hear a young evangelist named Greg Laurie and an intense musician named Keith Green.

As he sat in the unfamiliar surroundings of the sanctuary that evening, Hazen's analytical mind began to see this whole experience as a grand experiment. What if he were to walk forward at the evangelist's beckoning? What would he have to lose? What might he gain? And how could a budding scientist resist the chance to find out? Who says you can't put God in a test tube?

Now, here I was with Dr. Craig James Hazen, three-and-a-half decades later, as we sat in his book-lined office just off the campus of Biola University, a bastion of evangelical academia in La Mirada, California.

Pursuing his lifelong passion for science, he did go on to get his degree in biology at California State University, but he didn't stop there. He took a philosophical turn, unleashing his curiosity on the diverse religions around the world. He earned his master's degree and later his doctorate in religious studies at the University of California at Santa Barbara, and he is currently a professor at Biola, where he is also director of the master's degree program in science and religion.

Even in his fifties, he still has boyish looks and a contagious enthusiasm for discovery. His whimsical side continues to emerge on occasion — like the time he took a break from editing a major philosophical journal to pen the novel *Five Sacred Crossings*, in which he creatively uses fiction to explore spiritual themes.

I was on a trip to San Diego when I decided to drive north to Orange County and see Hazen, who seemed the ideal person to talk about two issues that I wanted to explore.

First, what about the good person, the law-abiding citizen, the one who plays by the rules and helps old ladies across the street and pays his taxes and declines tequila in favor of diet cola? Usually, the stories we hear are from ax-murderers-turned-missionaries, strippers-turned-Sunday-school-teachers, or abortionists who now march against *Roe v. Wade* — the astonishing tales of radical transformation that are the staple of Christian television. As inspiring as those accounts may be, what about the vast numbers of people who simply try to live decent lives — and generally succeed? How do they even come to the point of recognizing their need for grace?

And second, what about the billions of upstanding people around the planet who seek solace in other religious traditions? Is grace a universal component of faith, found in some permutation in every religion around the globe, or is this soul-liberating concept an exclusive offering of Christianity?

I figured that of all the people I knew, Craig Hazen — ever the researcher — would have answers.

Beyond Mercy to Grace

"Mercy and compassion — they pop up in virtually every religious tradition," Hazen was saying as he sat across from me at a round table flanked by shelves filled with academic books.

I nodded. "I've been looking into Islam," I said, "and even though Muslims see Allah as being stern and aloof, the Qur'an certainly talks about mercy and benevolence."

"That's true, but it's important to understand that the biblical conception of grace goes much farther than that," he said. "You see, in Christianity, God isn't just saying, 'I'm not going to punish you for what you've done.' That would be merciful, but he takes a dramatic next step by giving us something glorious — complete forgiveness and eternal life as a pure gift.

"It's like parents who catch their kids doing something wrong and they don't just let them off the hook, but they give them ice cream as well, because they love them so much," he said, flashing a smile. "That's what grace is — an amazing gift that we don't deserve and cannot earn or contribute to. It's lavish, it's undeserved, it's extravagant — it's unmerited favor that God bestows freely to those willing to receive it. We can't earn it, we can't contribute to it, we can't repay him for it, we can't take any credit for it, but God offers it because he made us in his image and wants to have a relationship with us for eternity. That's the Good News of the gospel. But to fully grasp it, we have to understand the bad news, as well."

"By 'bad news,' you mean sin," I said.

"That's right. You can't really have a robust concept of grace unless you really understand sin."

"And that," I said, "is a problem these days—many people have lost the concept of sin."

"Absolutely. Take the Mormons, for instance. They don't think there's a very big gap between human beings and God. In fact, they think humans and God are the same species—like, if you take enough vitamins and so on, then you can become a god," he said with a small chuckle.

"That's quite a contrast with Christianity."

"Yes, in Christianity, the gap that our sin creates between us and God is simply insurmountable. Trying to cross it is like jumping off the Newport Beach pier and trying to leap to Hawaii," he said, gesturing in the general direction of the Pacific Ocean.

"The first time, you don't get very far, so you train harder and harder," he continued. "You work with the best long jumpers in the world, you buy new athletic shoes, you lift weights, and you eat your spinach—and, oh my gosh, the next time you manage to jump twelve inches farther. Good for you! But the gap is still so huge. To overcome a divide that wide takes an almighty and all-loving being to provide a bridge, which God does through the cross of Christ. People don't understand that in our culture."

I mentioned that atheist comedian Ricky Gervais once claimed that he is "ten out of ten" in perfectly keeping God's commandments.[2]

"I thought that was reflective of our culture," I said. "People don't see themselves as being very bad, and therefore they don't appreciate the magnitude of this gift of grace that God is offering. Is that what you're saying?"

"Yeah, that's *the* disease today, especially in comfortable North America, where we've lost an understanding of the holiness of God," he replied. "Remember when Peter first met Jesus? Peter declared, 'Don't even gaze on me; I'm a sinful man!'[3] I don't think he had any inkling that this was the Son of God standing before him; he merely sensed that here was holiness, and he instantly understood that he was a wretched individual. Fortunately, there was a robust concept of sin in Judaism — you had to atone for it, year after year — and so there was at least that groundwork so he could understand it.

"Today, we don't have that groundwork," he said. "The self-esteem movement has taught us that *everybody's* great, *everybody* gets a trophy. People think, 'I'm no mass murderer, therefore I'm wonderful!' We've lost sight of the holiness of God and the depth of our own sin — and those are tough things to communicate to our culture."

"What do you say to people who don't think they need grace? How do you answer someone who says, 'I'm a nice person, I like God, I may not be religious, but I'm very spiritual'?"

Hazen thought for a moment. "There's a technique that evangelist Ray Comfort uses. He quizzes people on whether they've really lived according to the Ten Commandments. He asks, 'Have you ever lied?' And the person says, 'Hmmm, yeah.' Comfort says, 'Then you're a liar. Have you ever stolen anything?' They say, 'Well, yes.' And he says, 'Then you're a thief.' He goes through a litany of sins and gets people to admit they've been wicked in many respects, but they just haven't recognized it.

"That's one approach to helping people see their own sinfulness so they'll also understand their need for forgiveness and grace. It's hard to think seriously about grace until you understand that you've failed morally and will someday stand accountable before a holy God."

He shrugged. "Granted, Comfort's approach is a little bit in-your-face," he said. "But sometimes we have to find ways to sort of shake people by the existential nape of the neck."

Poster Boy for Grace

I pointed to the Bible on the table between us. "Which teaching of Jesus best crystalizes grace for you?"

Hazen was quick to respond. "It's got to be the story of the Prodigal Son.[4] It's over-the-top! It really does show how we're not just talking about mercy; we're talking about a God who's singularly focused on having a love relationship with us and is willing to do just about anything for that.

"In this parable, the son takes his inheritance and says, 'I'm going my own way.' The father probably took a deep breath and said, 'Oh, I hope one day he comes back!' And after a disastrous life that helps him realize the enormity of his sin, the son *does* come back—and scanning the horizon, the father sees him and without a moment of hesitation runs to him with a ring, sandals, and a feast. The father doesn't just begrudgingly allow his son secondary status as a disfavored servant, but he orders a party in his honor and reinstates him as his child."

Hazen's eyebrows shot up. "Wow!" he exclaimed. "What a story of undeserved favor! You don't find anything like that in the other religions of the world."

"Are you sure?" I asked. "I thought there was a story in Buddhist literature that parallels the Prodigal Son parable."

"Well, they're similar to the degree that they both involve sons who rebelled and left home, then later saw the error of their ways and came back. But the Buddhist story ends quite differently—the son has to work off his misdeeds."

"How?"

"He ends up toiling for twenty-five years, hauling dung. So that provides a stark contrast between the God of grace and a religion where people have to work their way to nirvana."[5]

A feast with the fatted calf versus hauling piles of dung—yes, quite a difference, I mused. "What about Islam?" I asked. "How would the Prodigal Son story play out there?"

"In my view, it's just not possible for a parable like that to emerge from Islamic circles," Hazen said. "I'm not sure the prodigal son would ever come back. Family shame is very significant in Islam. The family's honor is a reflection of the way the family submits to Allah. The level of shame in the young man leaving his family would have been intolerable."

"And if he *did* come back?"

"He'd be on his hands and knees before Allah, and there would be great penance to pay—*if* that. No, the prodigal son is a product of Christian theology, which is a wellspring of grace, forgiveness, and hope. You find the Prodigal Son story coming from the lips of Jesus —and nobody else."

My hand swept the array of books on Hazen's bookshelves. "You've spent your academic life studying the religions of the world. Are you saying that grace is nowhere else to be found?"

"The Christian view of grace sets it apart from all the other great religions, there's no question about it. Having said that, though, there is at least a sense of grace in a couple of other traditions," he replied.

"What groups come closest?"

"One would be the cat school of *bhakti* Hinduism."

I looked up from my notes. "I'm sorry—did you say the *cat* school?"

"That's right. The name comes from the image of how a mother cat uses her teeth to gently carry her kitten to its destination. The kitten can't do anything on its own; all the effort comes from the mother. So the idea in this branch of Hinduism is that you're fully dependent on the deity's discretion to carry you to enlightenment or deliverance from karma. That's a picture of grace, but it's much different than Christianity."

"How so?"

"First and foremost, it's not real. Christianity is a historical faith, rooted in reality. Second, it lacks the Christian concept of a personal God. And third, you can't have a robust theology of grace without a concept of sin from which you're being saved, and essentially that's missing in Hinduism."

"What other tradition has hints of grace?" I asked.

"There's the *Jodo Shinshu* school of Buddhism, where the only hope of getting to enlightenment is through the gift of the Amida Buddha. This was developed as far back as the twelfth century and was reengaged in the fifteenth century."

"So it postdates Christianity?"

"Yes, that's true. So does the cat school, for that matter. And again, the Christian concept of grace — with the holiness of a personal God, the reality of sin, the historical grounding — is much different. In the end," he said, "Christianity is unique. Its teachings on grace are unparalleled in world religions. In short, the Prodigal Son is still the poster boy for grace."

The Son Who Wasn't a Prodigal

Some people are in obvious need of God's forgiveness — like the brutal slave trader John Newton, who ended up so amazed by grace that he penned the classic hymn about it, or Saul of Tarsus, a persecutor of Christians who celebrated grace after he became the apostle Paul. But then there are the Craig Hazens of the world — the sons who never were prodigals, the nice guys whose veneer of morality seems to be polished a little brighter than the norm.

"How did you come to the point of recognizing your need for grace?" I asked.

"When I was a senior in high school, I was a smart kid, and everyone thought I was going somewhere," he said. "My family life was okay; my parents were divorced, but I was on the straight and narrow. I remember looking around as I became aware of the cosmos, and saying, *What's this all about?* I was coming to the conclusion that since most religious views don't hold any water—"

"You were a skeptic?"

"Yeah, a village agnostic. No Christian had ever offered me good reasons to believe, so I was basically coming to the conclusion that the world is probably all about me. Then a girl invited me to hear an evangelist at a church. I remember the message—it was based on the fourth chapter of John, where Jesus offers the Samaritan woman 'living water' that leads to eternal life.[6] I figured, *What do I have to lose?* I walked forward at the altar call, but frankly it was just an experiment at the time."

"What happened then?"

"They took me to a side room for counseling. I thought, *Uh-oh, this is where the brainwashing takes place.* Before long, all the counselors were clustered around me because I was peppering them with questions that nobody could answer."

"So you walked out that night unconvinced?"

"Pretty much, but I had started a journey. They began giving me books and tapes and following up with phone calls. I studied the issues for several months, and finally, doggone it, God sealed it. I became convinced Christianity is true.

"And then I began to understand why I'd been attracted to the peace that I had seen in my chemistry teacher—the one who kept putting God posters on the walls. Even though I was a good kid, I was still a sinner, and I was experiencing a sense of anxiety and alienation that I couldn't quite put my finger on. God began to deal with that in my life.

"In fact," he continued, "here's a funny thing about grace. A couple of years later, evangelists came to the college I was attending and brought some guys who had dramatic testimonies. They stood on the cement planter in the quad and told about how they had been in the gutter and did all kinds of horrible things, yet the Lord found them and lifted them up. And I was thinking, 'Man, I want to jump up there too, but I want to give a different testimony.' You see, I *wasn't* in the gutter, I *wasn't* the dregs of society, I had great promise, everybody thought I was on the road to success. And guess what? I still desperately needed God!

"Here's what I came to understand: having good table manners, getting A's in school, saying 'please' and 'thank you' and being nice to people—that's all pretty trivial stuff. Actually, I was in rebellion against a Holy God so powerful that he could speak billions of galaxies into existence. Now, that's *huge*! I was ignoring him, I was turning my back on him, and my sins—my pride, my smugness, my selfishness, and all of my secret deceit and illicit desires—had created an enormous gap between us, and it was fostering that sense of alienation and anxiety in me.

"That's what sin does. God is perfect, he is holy, he is pure—and I certainly wasn't, neither in thought nor deed. The Bible stresses that nobody is truly good—Romans 3:23 says that 'all have sinned and fall short of the glory of God.' Over time, I came to realize that the plain language of that verse means what it explicitly says—'all have sinned,' and that includes me.

"I needed forgiveness, and I found grace through Jesus."

Of Flies and Flour Mills

The story of God's grace has been enshrined in music, embedded in Scripture, and extolled by millions of people who have been overcome with gratitude for forgiveness and eternal life. It has been the subject of poetry, paintings, and literature—but is it the stuff of logic? Ultimately, does it make sense? I asked Hazen for his opinion—and I got a logical response.

"From one perspective, no, grace is too over-the-top to be logical," he said. "And yet from another angle, it does make good sense. For example, Philip Yancey points out that if you raise a child with conditional love, then you will end up with a neurotic and insecure child.[7] And if God were to make his love conditional on how well we perform and keep his rules, we'd become neurotic as well.

"Psychologists will tell you that if the goal is to have human beings flourish, then unconditional love has to be part of the package. If the system were set up so that you had to earn your way to God, you wouldn't know how much you need to do or whether you'd made it or not, and you would live in a terrible state of anxiety."

An illustration I had heard years earlier popped into my mind. "It would be like a salesman being told by his boss that he must meet his quota or be fired—but then never letting him know what the quota was," I said.

"Exactly. For example, Islam is based on earning your way to God by doing more good deeds than bad ones. Officially, Muslims can't know if they've pleased Allah, and consequently they must constantly strive to do everything they can to pile up the good deeds."

"So what happens?" I asked.

"Let me give you an example from an influential Muslim leader concerning the month of Ramadan, when Muslims are required to fast. He was speculating about different scenarios that might interrupt the fast. He was very concerned about this, because when all is said and done, he wanted his good deeds to outweigh his bad deeds, so at least he had a shot of making it to paradise.

"The Muslim leader speculated: suppose a man is sitting in a chair during Ramadan and falls asleep. His head cocks back, his mouth falls open. A fly comes through an open window and darts into his mouth and out again. Has the fast been nullified? He analyzes this situation and similar ones for several pages—like, what if dust gets in your mouth? Well, could you have anticipated there would be dust in the air? Did you know that you would be driving on a dusty road? What kind of dust was it? Was it dust from the road or from a flour mill? All of these appear to be very important considerations.

"He goes on, page after page, and by the end you sort of collapse in exhaustion—all the things you've got to track in order to make sure that day's fast gets fully credited so you've got a possibility of going to paradise. Now, do all Muslims live that way? No, of course not, and yet if they really take the Qur'an's teachings seriously, they're pushed toward this kind of mindset."

Hazen threw up his hands and sat back in his chair. "Oh, my goodness, give me grace!" he declared. "Give me the father of the Prodigal Son! He is our only hope."

Five Pillars of Islam

Of all the world religions outside of Christianity, Islam intrigues me the most. "Without any real theology of grace, how does Islam provide salvation to Muslims?" I asked.

"Muhammad spelled out rituals that Muslims are required to perform. They're called the five pillars," Hazen replied. "There's the confession, or *shahada*—where they must affirm with true intention that there is no god but Allah and that Muhammad is his messenger. This is how Muslims are converted. Second, they're required to participate in prayer rituals five times a day, following certain customs like ceremonial washing and facing the Kaaba, a sacred building in Mecca.

"Third is almsgiving, where two-and-a-half percent of eligible assets are given to mosques or Islamic charities. Fourth, it's required that Muslims fast for thirty days, from sunrise to sunset, during the ninth month of the lunar calendar, which is called Ramadan. Finally, those who have the physical and financial means are required to go on the *hajj*, a pilgrimage to Mecca, Muhammad's birthplace, at least once during their lifetime."

"And if they do all these things faithfully, then they're assured of paradise?"

"Well, not exactly. Traditionally, Muslims have believed that each of them is watched at all times by two angels, one on each shoulder. The angel on the right records the person's good deeds; the one on the left, his bad ones. On the day of judgment, those deeds are weighed on a balance."

"And if the good exceeds the bad, they go to heaven?"

"That's up to Allah. You see, there's no guarantee he will honor the scales. It's entirely up to him whether or not he will offer mercy. There are only two ways you can be absolutely sure of paradise: either dying in Mecca during a pilgrimage or in battle for the cause of Allah."

"A *jihad*?"

"A *jihad* can mean any struggle for God's sake, but a holy war is the highest form of jihad."[8]

"Then there's no real atonement for sin in Islam as there is in Christianity?"

"No, the Qur'an specifically says no soul can bear the sins of another soul."[9]

"So Islam is essentially a system of trying to please God, and yet nobody can have confidence that they've done enough to warrant paradise," I said.

"That's right. Now, I've met Muslims who say they don't focus on the rituals. They believe everybody needs to do good in this world, and they say they want to serve Allah. Not necessarily *love* Allah, but serve him and do what's right before him.

"But given the nature of Allah, you can't even hope that you'll ever be saved. In fact, it's arrogant to claim that you are a Muslim, which means someone who has submitted to Allah, because you can't honestly know if you're fully in that state. It's very much works based, although mercy can come at the end when Allah makes the final call. So you're on a treadmill of performance your whole life. And to me, that's the worst of all worlds—striving to achieve something and never really knowing if you've done it or are even close to it."

I asked, "Why would the 9/11 terrorists do things flagrantly against Islamic rules—like going to strip clubs and drinking alcohol—before they flew airliners into the Pentagon and World Trade Center? Weren't they concerned this would weigh against them in the judgment?"

"No, because there's a mindset that says, *I'm tired of working harder and faster to tip those scales in my favor, so I'm going to do one big act that's going to tip them for all eternity—and that will be an act of* jihad. *Consequently, it doesn't matter what I do in the days leading up to this, because this final act will tip the scales decisively.* That way, they can justify the violations of all kinds of Islamic rules and dictates."

I could see how that made some sense within the Islamic framework—a performance-driven theology without grace, without the assurance of salvation, without a loving relationship between a Father and the children he has created. A world, in sum, where the Prodigal Son would have had a far different fate.

Polar Opposite of Christianity

From Islam, I turned our conversation to Eastern religions. "What about mainstream Buddhism?" I asked. "Do you see any trace of grace there?"

"Buddhism is primarily atheistic," Hazen said. "There might be gods in the system at certain points, but we just use them to climb to higher levels, and then even those gods disappear. Ultimately, there's nothing, and you have no soul, so there's no real concept of sin or grace."

"So, if a Buddhist were sitting here, what would he make of our conversation?"

"He would probably say, 'Ah, that's wonderful—the concept of sin and grace.'"

That surprised me. "Really?"

"Sure. What he would mean is that for you—where you're at on your spiritual journey—those concepts are meaningful, and they're helping you climb the ladder. But once you get up the ladder, those concepts will disappear as you become mindful of other levels and ultimately the mindfulness that you don't exist and you have no soul. Now you're really heading to nirvana, where in the end you'll be absorbed into nothingness."

"Most Westerners see Buddhism as being a lot of meditation, but actually it's a lot of hard work, isn't it?"

"Yes, any serious Buddhist would know that you have to follow the eight-fold path to move toward the cessation of suffering—right understanding, right intention, right speech, right action, right livelihood, right effort, right mindfulness, and right concentration, or meditation. You have to watch your behavior constantly because that's part of moving toward enlightenment. You might be on that wheel of *samsara* for a long time, going through a cycle of births and rebirths as you work toward liberation."

"How long might that cycle last?"

"According to Buddhist thinkers, the fewest number of lifetimes you could work through this would be seven—and almost nobody does it that quickly," he said. "It's more like a million lifetimes, or I heard one Buddhist teacher say it was one times ten to the sixtieth power of lifetimes. That's starting to approach the number of atoms in the observable universe! Can you imagine that? That would be the number of cycles that you would have to go through before you're thrown into nirvana."

"That's staggering!"

Hazen nodded. "In a sense Buddhism is the polar opposite of Christianity," he said. "Ultimately, nothing exists in Buddhism; in Christianity, ultimately God is the Creator. In Buddhism, you don't have a soul; in Christianity, you have a soul that's made in God's image. In Buddhism, you have a seemingly endless slog ahead of you to reach nirvana; in Christianity, forgiveness and eternal life in heaven are a free gift of God's grace that we can receive at any time through repentance and faith. In Buddhism, there's no such thing as sin; ultimately, there's just substancelessness, or *nihsvabhava*, to use the Sanskrit term."

Hazen thought for a moment, then concluded: "You know, even if all religions were figments of our imagination, I would choose Christianity, because it says you can be assured that you're right with God. There's no need for performance anxiety or laboring through lifetime after lifetime. As the Bible says in 1 John 5:13: 'I write these things to you who believe in the name of the Son of God so that you may *know* that you have eternal life.' "[10]

Knocking at Your Door

When I was growing up in the homogenized Chicago suburbs of the 1950s and 1960s, religions like Islam, Hinduism, and Buddhism seemed foreign and exotic; today, our nation is so diverse that I've got numerous faiths represented in my own neighborhood. But only adherents of two of them — Jehovah's Witnesses and Mormonism — have come knocking at my front door.

"Both these faiths claim to be Christian," I said to Hazen, "and yet their teachings contradict key Christian doctrines. Let's start with Jehovah's Witnesses — how do they view grace?"

"Jehovah's Witnesses deny the unique deity of Jesus — they believe he is *a* god, not the second person of the Trinity — and their teachings conflict with the biblical notion of grace. They do believe in a certain form of saving faith, but they also believe it has to be connected with some significant hard work. You've got to put in your time and do what's required of you—serving at the Kingdom Hall, going door-to-door through neighborhoods, and so forth."

My mind flashed to an image of Hazen greeting Jehovah's Witnesses on his front porch, and I had to stifle a grin. "They probably get a surprise when they drop in on you," I said.

"I'll tell you a story about that," he said. "I have an office upstairs in my house that overlooks the street, and one day I saw a van pull up. Some people got out with little briefcases, and they fanned out. Two of them started moving around my neighborhood. It was a nice day, and so they were sauntering. Certainly they weren't moving very fast as they went from door-to-door.

"Finally, they knocked on my door, and I struck up a conversation. I told them that contrary to what Jehovah Witnesses believe, I'm convinced we're saved by the grace of God alone. They said, 'Oh, no, you've got to work hard to do that. The very fact that we're out in the neighborhood right now—this is part of it. The easy salvation that you folks talk about just doesn't ring true for us.'

"I said, 'Well, I have an office upstairs, and I saw you going around the neighborhood. And honestly, ladies, this isn't to criticize you, but, wow, you seemed like you could have covered at least twice as many houses in the same amount of time. Don't you care about Jehovah and his message? It seems to me that if you really cared, you could have covered two, maybe three times as many houses to get the word out.'

"It was very effective with them, because it crystalized one of the big problems with a works-based mentality: if you're going to live by works, you're going to end up dying by those works. How are you going to stand before Jehovah and say, 'Yeah, I could have worked a lot harder'? You never would know if you've done enough for him, because ultimately it's based on you.

"While they claim grace is involved in their system, it's a hybrid

—which is actually contradictory when you think about real grace," Hazen said. "Genuine grace is the free gift of salvation—and you can't add a price to something that's already free."

Grace — After All You Can Do

"We certainly see a works-based mentality in Mormonism," I observed. "I was perusing a Book of Mormon that I found in my hotel room last night, and I came across 2 Nephi 25:23, which says, "... for we know that it is by grace that we are saved, after all we can do.'"[11]

"By and large, the Latter-day Saints (LDS), or Mormons, believe exactly that. There are a lot of things they have to do—and then God hopefully will cover over the rest. That means they need to be faithful, they need to tithe, they need to do temple work, they need to be married in the temple, they need to serve, and they really ought to be going on their mission. There's an abiding sense of guilt or failure if they miss any of those.

"Now, when I talk to the folks at Brigham Young University, many of them are very focused on grace. They'll say you're saved by grace after all that you can do—and then they'll say, 'What is all that you can do?' They turn to another passage in the *Book of Mormon*, Alma 24:11, where it basically says that all you can do is repent.[12] This sounds a lot more traditionally Christian."

"Are some Mormon leaders moving more toward a grace-based theology?"

"Yes, I believe so, but in a nuanced way—and I hope this will develop further."

"As it stands now, though, the average Mormon would see a list of do's that they have to cross off their list in order to feel like they're getting right with God," I said.

"Yes, that's the strong tradition."

"Can they ever have confidence that they are okay with God?"

"It's mixed. Many feel pretty secure in their relationship with God. In fact, some Mormons I've met may very well be saved. They understand Jesus accurately in several respects and love him with all their heart, and they really do believe they're saved by the merits of Christ alone — despite the burdensome tradition of works righteousness that Mormonism has offered. But there are many who are insecure about their salvation and their standing in the LDS church, and statistics bear that out. The youth culture in Utah has consistently had a suicide rate that is well above average for the country, and some people attribute it to the guilt that comes along with the behavioral standards of Mormonism. There can be a lot of despair."[13]

I shook my head. "That's tragic."

"Yes, it is, and I think we, as evangelicals, can resonate with that. Sometimes we see guilt and shame in our own movement when we're too legalistic, and it can send people down a very dark road. By the way," he added, "there's something else about Mormon salvation that's often missed."

"What's that?"

"Essentially, Mormonism is a universalistic faith — according to their theology, everybody gets saved in some sense. Mormons believe that whether you're a believer or not, the atonement ensures that you will be resurrected and you will go to one of the heavens."

"Heavens? Plural?"

"Yes, Mormons believe in three heavens, or what they call *degrees of glory.* The lowest would be the *Telestial Kingdom*, then the *Terrestrial Kingdom*, and finally the *Celestial Kingdom*. So when you're talking about grace, you have to understand these nuances.

"You see, the atonement basically boosts everybody into one of these heavens. There are a few people, called the sons of perdition, who face a special quarantine area, a kind of hell. But by and large, everybody gets into one of the heavens. Now, I don't know about you, but if I'm going to live for eternity in a heaven, I want the top level, where you have direct access to the presence of God himself."

"How do Mormons believe you get there?"

"The answer is there's a lot of work to do. The demands can be quite burdensome. You've got to follow all the rituals and customs of the church and store up a lot of good works. In fact, here's what I say to Mormons at my door. They tell me that I need to be a Mormon in order to spend eternity with God, and I reply, 'I'm a Christian, and from my standpoint there are two places: heaven and hell. From your LDS perspective, where would I go?'

"They say, 'Well, you seem to be a decent guy and a Jesus lover, uh, there's a good chance you're going to the second level of heaven.' I ask, 'What's that like?' They say, 'Oh, it's more glorious than you can possibly imagine.' I say, 'Hmmm. So if I'm wrong and you're right, I get to go to a place that's more glorious than I can possibly imagine. But if I choose the Mormon faith and it's wrong, I may very well end up in hell for eternity. Consequently, it makes no sense for me to become a Mormon.'"

I smiled at this apologetic jujitsu. "The bottom line," I said, "is that Mormonism contradicts traditional Christian teaching in numerous ways."

"In my view, Mormonism is not Christian because it differs on a number of essential teachings. Maybe the most important difference is simply that Christianity is monotheistic," Hazen said. "Mormon theology teaches that there are at least three separate Gods—the Father, Son, and Holy Spirit—and historically Mormons have been radical polytheists, thinking that any male in proper standing with the LDS church will become a god himself. That means there may be innumerable gods out there. No matter how you slice it, that's *not* Christianity."

A Faith That Can Be Tested

Hazen's analysis of other religions led me to a related question. I told him I have encountered some astounding stories of people who have found grace through Christ and their lives have been radically transformed as a result. In fact, I'm an example of that, as are several people I have interviewed for this book.

"And yet, there are Muslims, Hindus, and members of other religions who claim they've been fundamentally changed for the better because of their faith," I said. "So how does a transformed life count for the truth of Christianity—or does it?"

"On the one hand," replied Hazen, "I've seen examples of people who have been so personally revolutionized that I can only attribute it to the work of Christ. So, yes, I believe that a Christian's testimony about the power of God in their life can be persuasive to a degree, though it needs to be combined with other evidence to really make the case for Christianity.

"On the other hand, people in other religions also claim to have meaningful religious experiences. I remember teaching a class on world religions at the University of California at Santa Barbara, and we all drove to Los Angeles to tour religious sites. At the Krishna Temple, they invited us to observe their worship. They had tambourines and drums, and they were chanting and dancing. Afterward, an evangelical student seemed bothered. He said, 'I'm having trouble seeing the difference between what they do and what we do. It *felt* the same.'

"As I explained to this student, it's true that people in other religious movements can have wonderful experiences that make them feel spiritually uplifted. In fact, good feelings can be generated in so many different ways that we ought not let our feelings dictate which religious direction we're going to go.

"Yes, you want to be transformed by your faith, but you also want to know that it's the real deal. So while grace sets apart Christianity, so does truth. Jesus was filled with grace *and* truth, and in Christianity you can *know* the truth, not just through some sort of spiritual experience, but also through careful investigation.

"In other words, Christianity can be tested. And when you check it out—as I know that you did, Lee, when you were an atheist—you find that it's supported by philosophy, science, and history; in fact, Christianity makes the most sense of the world. No other religion lines up with reality as Christianity does.

"In 1 Corinthians 15:12–19, Paul says twice that if Jesus did not come back from the dead, our faith is worthless. He was saying that you can actually investigate Christianity, and if you don't have excellent reasons to believe that Jesus came back from the dead, then you're well within your rights to move on to something else. Other religions don't open themselves for that kind of investigation and scrutiny of their claims.

"Actually, some faiths don't even think about such things. If you're a Zen Buddhist, for example, what's important to you? Well, through meditative practices and disciplines, are you moving closer to enlightenment? At the end of the day, the Zen Buddhist doesn't really care whether the Buddha actually existed or whether he taught the four noble truths and the eight-fold path—it's all about what's going on *inside* of him. So a lot of religions don't even claim to be true in any objective sense. Then there are some other religions—and I would put Mormonism and Islam in this category—that sound like they're historical, but when you drill down a little it turns out they're not."

"What do you mean by that?" I asked.

"The Mormon missionary at your door might do a presentation about Joseph Smith restoring 'true' Christianity. He may talk about gold plates upon which reformed Egyptian characters were inscribed and how Smith translated these by the power of God. He may tell a grand story about Jesus visiting the Western Hemisphere. And you'd be thinking, 'Wow, a person can actually investigate some of this and weigh whether or not it's true.'

"But let's say you've done your homework about flaws in their case and you raise a few of the many legitimate objections. What happens? Invariably, the missionary says, 'You're making some good points, but ultimately it doesn't matter that you have those objections, because I've had an experience that tells me this is true.' He will tell you to simply read the Book of Mormon and see if you have a 'burning in your bosom' that confirms it. So what initially sounded like a faith that could be investigated suddenly becomes one that is based on feelings.

"Islam is similar. I've had discussions with Muslims about the identity of Jesus, and they will describe him as he appears in the Qur'an. I tell them, 'I don't think that's accurate, because the very best records we have of Jesus push right back into the first century, and it seems to me we ought to trust those. After all, they were written by people with knowledge of these events, and they wrote very early.'

"The Muslim will reply, 'There's one problem: the Qur'an is the Word of Allah.' I'll insist that we talk about the evidence—the best historical data about Jesus—but again they'll say I'm missing the point: the Qur'an is the Word of Allah. You see, for them everything stops with that assertion—there are no arguments, nor is there any evidence that can possibly count against it. That's a far cry from Christianity, where apologists like to start with the reliability of historical documents. So Christianity is different, first, because of grace; second, because it's testable; and third, because it paints a picture that matches the way the world is, in a way that other religions don't."

"That third one's a big statement. Give me an example."

"Sure—consider the problem of evil, pain, and suffering. Christians approach this by affirming that these are real and explaining that Christianity offers a cogent explanation for their existence.[14] If you move into Eastern religious traditions, almost every one of them renames evil, pain, and suffering as *maya*, or illusion."

"That sort of brushes them off the table, doesn't it?" I said.

"Yes, and it doesn't comport with reality," he replied. "The picture painted by Christianity matches the way the world really is. We are called as Christians to help people who are suffering, not dismiss their suffering as an illusion and thereby minimize or dismiss it.

"What I'm saying is this: Christianity—in so many key areas—reflects reality in a way that other faiths simply do not."

Cacophony of Religions

Our discussion prompted a verse to jump into my mind: "For the law was given through Moses; grace and truth came through Jesus Christ."[15] As Hazen said, both grace and truth are important—*grace* opens the door to a relationship with God through no merit of our own, and yet it's merely wishful thinking unless Christianity is based on *truth*. It is, to use Hazen's phrase, a testable faith. As my colleague Mark Mittelberg likes to say, the arrows of science, history, and philosophy point powerfully and persuasively toward the truthfulness of Christian theism.[16]

My cell phone buzzed, signaling my need to end our conversation so I could drive to San Diego for another meeting. I packed up my recording gear and thanked Hazen for his time as we stood to shake hands.

"Honestly," he said with that boyish smile, "there's nothing I enjoy discussing more than grace. It's an inexhaustible topic."

Over the next ninety minutes, as I drove in my rental car through the snarled roadways of Southern California, there were signs of a diverse religious culture everywhere—the woman in the hijab pushing a stroller down the sidewalk; the statue of Buddha in the window of a Vietnamese café; the driver wearing a yarmulke in the car next to mine; the tidy Kingdom Halls of the Jehovah's Witnesses; the massive stone Mormon Temple, its spires reaching heavenward, that looms next to the freeway in San Diego. So many beliefs, each with their demands and rules and requirements and expectations — to-do lists that never quite get completed.

And everywhere I drove, atop Lutheran, Episcopal, Methodist, and Baptist churches, both traditional and modern, crosses rose toward the sky — not just a reminder of the unique message of freely offered grace, but so much more than that: a symbol of the unimaginable cost that was required to purchase it.

CHAPTER 5

The Executioner

Are We Ever Beyond the Reach of Grace?

To be a Christian means to forgive the inexcusable,
because God has forgiven the inexcusable in you.
C. S. Lewis[1]

A carefree youngster playing in a prince's palace. A reign of terror that splits the boy's family apart. An odyssey through fields of mayhem and death. A life mysteriously spared. A stranger with a shadowy past. A monster of unthinkable depravity—and a personal transformation so improbable that it seemingly stretches the concept of grace to its breaking point.

Christopher LaPel's story sounds like a Hollywood film. The tale begins with a Cambodian child's innocent request of a royal craftsman. Then it winds through a bewildering maze of horrors before ending in a dungeon with no hope of escape, occupied by a prisoner with no hope except Christ.

I had come a long way in piecing together the riddle of grace. Stephanie Fast reminded me how God's grace doesn't just forgive us; it clears the way for us to be adopted into his very family for eternity. Jud Wilhite, snatched by God from the verge of self-destruction, cautioned against trying to prove we're worthy of grace even after we've received it as an unmerited gift. And Craig Hazen affirmed that in a world of religions in which God is seen as a relentless taskmaster, Christianity stands alone as a beacon of grace.

But what are the boundaries of grace? Where does God draw the line? Surely there must be limits — reprehensible monsters whose ghastly transgressions extend far beyond the redemptive shadow of the cross. If there were ever a case of grace going too far, where God shakes his head and turns his back, I knew it would be found in the story told by Christopher LaPel.

Not long after I returned home from my visit with Hazen, I caught a flight back to the West Coast to seek out LaPel (pronounced *La-PELL*), whose Los Angeles office features a bulletin board festooned with newspaper clippings about his exploits.

Diminutive and wearing rimless glasses, his hair black with no gray, LaPel sat casually in a wooden chair, his ankles crossed, as he calmly told me a riveting tale of sadism and survival.

"I grew up in Phnom Penh, Cambodia, where my father was a high priest and spiritual advisor to Prince Norodom Sihanouk," he said, his voice heavily accented and his sentences clipped.

"My dad wanted me to take his position someday. When I was young, sometimes he would take me to the palace, where I would play with the prince's children. One day I was in the basement and saw some craftsmen. I said, 'Would you make me a cross out of ivory?'"

"A cross?" I asked. "Why would a Buddhist child ask for a cross?"

"I don't really know why. Maybe it was because I used to see one on a Catholic church. My siblings had idols, but for some reason I was fixated on getting a cross. To me, it represented power and purity. The craftsman made the cross, and I put it on a gold chain. It hung right here, under my shirt," he said, tapping his heart.

"How did your father react?"

"Nobody could see it — until one day we were eating a meal as a family. We would sit on the floor with food in the center. When I reached to get something, the cross fell out of my shirt. Everyone looked. My dad was angry — he cursed at me in front of my brothers and sisters. He pulled me toward him and said, 'You shouldn't wear that cross! Remember, we are a Buddhist family.'"

"Did he punish you?"

"Afterward, he apologized, but he said he didn't like the cross. He offered to make me any idol I wanted. I said, 'No, I don't want anything else.' Then he said, 'Next time, take it off.' After that, I moved the cross from my front to my back."

LaPel was wearing the cross on April 17, 1975, when the Khmer Rouge took over and forcibly emptied Cambodia's towns and cities. "They burst in with AK-47s and said, 'You have to leave as soon as possible. Don't take anything. In three days, you will come back.'"

He and his family joined a flood of residents who clogged the narrow roads—walking, running, some riding bicycles and motor scooters, carrying everything they could. There was mass confusion and panic.

"Everyone was scared. I was nineteen at the time. I was terrified. My dad said, 'Just do what they ask.' Three days turned into three weeks. Then we realized—we would never get back home."

So began their quest to avoid the Killing Fields.

Mystery of the Cross

Over the next 1,364 days, the Khmer Rouge, seeking to obliterate the social classes and create an agrarian society of peasants, was responsible for killing, starving, or working to death about two million Cambodians, out of a population of eight million. Accounting for the percentage of people destroyed, Pol Pot's Communist regime was the most murderous in the modern age.

"Teachers—dead. Former government workers—dead. Journalists—dead," LaPel said to me. "They wanted to get rid of anyone who was educated, so they would not be a threat. A friend of mine admitted to the Khmer Rouge that he was in college. He disappeared."

In fact, out of 11,000 university students at the time, only 450 survived. Just five percent of secondary students lived through the genocide. As for physicians, nine out of ten perished.[2] Money was abolished, personal property confiscated, schools shuttered, courts closed, religious practices suppressed, individuality eradicated, and masses of people were driven into the rice paddies to be used as slave labor.[3]

"There was to be no love except love for the Organization and the nation," said one journalist.[4]

In other words, it was an entire culture without grace.

"The Khmer Rouge would question us," LaPel said. "We had to be careful—one slip and we were dead. They would say, 'Who are you? Have you been to school?' They shoved a notebook in front of us. 'Here—write your name.'

"I wrote my name with my left hand, so it looked awkward. I said I was a farmer with just a couple years of school. They tested us: 'If you want to raise beans, what do you do?' In Phnom Penh, we would plant some corn and vegetables, so we knew a little. We were able to convince them we were farmers."

Separated from his family, LaPel was put to work in the fields to grow rice and build canals as part of a grand strategy to construct a massive irrigation system and increase rice production. He worked twelve to fourteen hours a day; at night in the summer, he toiled by moonlight. Food was a watery soup, supplemented by lizards he would catch. His weight dropped to ninety pounds; his hair was falling out from malnutrition. At night, the Khmer Rouge would call out names and people would disappear from their huts, never to be seen again.

"Sometime in late 1977, I got very sick with a high fever," LaPel told me. "I missed three days of work. One night, a voice called out my name. It was the Khmer Rouge—they wanted to see me. They dragged me from my hut. That was it—I knew I would be killed. I was scared, I was trembling.

"They told me to sit on the floor, and they asked me why I hadn't been working. I told them I was sick but had no food or medicine.

One said, 'What kind of sick are you?' I said, 'I have a high fever.' Someone said, 'Let's see how sick you are.'

"They began checking me. One put his hand on my head; another, on my shoulder. Then one opened my shirt to put his hand on my chest—and that exposed the cross, hanging by a string. The light reflected off the ivory. There was silence, it seemed, for a long time. Then there was a voice from somebody I couldn't see. He said, 'Well, this guy is really sick. We'll let him go.'"

I was inching toward the edge of my seat as LaPel told the story. "Thank God!" I said. "But why did they react that way to the cross?"

"I don't know why. They told me to go rest. The next day they gave me Chinese medicine and rice soup and treated me very well. A few days later, I got better. I don't know what it was about that cross, but I believe it saved my life."

Still, the struggle to stay alive in the rice fields became increasingly difficult. The workload increased as the food supply diminished. The brutality of the Khmer Rouge was relentless; LaPel was anguished by hearing people begging for their lives before they were executed.

LaPel weighed his options and decided he had nothing to lose by fleeing. In early 1979 he made a dash for the safety of Thailand. He escaped at night, navigating the jungle by moonlight, and eventually arrived at a refugee camp that was called by a name he didn't quite understand: Christian Outreach.

"I was so relieved, so happy to be there," he said. "I felt safe for the first time in so long. Then one day a woman shared with me about Jesus Christ. She talked about how he had died on the cross—and I thought, *The cross?* I said, 'Tell me the meaning of the cross. Why did he die?' She told me about how he died so I could be saved from my sins.

"At that moment, I remembered my ivory cross and how God saved my life when I was sick. I prayed, 'Lord, I was supposed to die that night, but you spared me. I want to commit my life to serving you, no matter what you want me to do. My life is yours.' "

He went to feel the cross around his neck, but it was gone. Somewhere in the jungle, the string had broken. He grinned at the memory. "I had lost my cross," he said, "but I had found Jesus."

It was in the camp where LaPel met and fell in love with another refugee named Vanna, and they were married. In 1980 they immigrated to the United States, where Vanna had a sister. LaPel graduated from a school fittingly named Hope International University and became pastor of Golden West Christian Church in Los Angeles, located on a street called Liberty. That's where I met with him in his second-floor office.

LaPel has never forgotten Cambodia. He has continued to go back and forth to his homeland to train and equip Christians. Today, more than two hundred churches can trace their origins back to his ministry.

The Horror of S-21

Other members of LaPel's family were not as fortunate. When he talks about their fate, his voice becomes softer and softer; at times, I had to strain to hear him.

While he was still held captive in Cambodia, he explained, he got word that the Khmer Rouge had worked his father and mother to death. His sister, who was a broadcaster in the capital city, was slain. His brother was killed shortly before the Vietnamese intervened in 1979.

"Then there was my cousin ...," he said.

"Tell me about her."

He hesitated. "She was a scientist who taught at a school." Pause. "She was arrested and taken to S-21."

The notorious S-21 was the former Tuol Svay Pray High School just outside of Phnom Penh. The compound had four three-story buildings, all facing a grass courtyard, and a wooden administrative building. In 1976 the Khmer Rouge converted the complex into an interrogation, torture, and execution center. The "S" stood for *sala*, which meant "hall," and the "21" was the code for *santebal*, or security police.[5]

Those living nearby only knew the facility as *konlaenh choul min dael chenh*—"the place where people go in but never come out."[6] Every prisoner was deemed guilty of treason when he or she entered; in fact, the traditional Cambodian term for prisoner, *neak thos*, literally means "guilty person."[7]

Said one historian, "Like Joseph K in Kafka's novel *The Trial*, they had not been accused because they were guilty; they were guilty because they had been accused."[8] A Khmer Rouge slogan summed up their strategy: "Better to destroy ten innocent people than to let one enemy go free."[9]

Kaing Guek Eav, whose *nom de guerre* was Comrade Duch (pronounced *Doik*), a former mathematics teacher, presided over the institution with brutal bureaucratic efficiency.[10] With chilling precision, he compiled documentation of every torture session, every forced confession, every murder.

All prisoners were photographed when they arrived. On a list of eight teenagers and nine children, Duch wrote the order: "Kill them all." On another order, he wrote, "Use the hot method, even if it kills him." His notations for other prisoners included "take away for execution," "keep for interrogation," or "medical experiment."[11]

Sometimes the S-21 torturers would compel confessions by hanging prisoners upside down, their head in a bucket of urine and feces. Other times, electric shocks, suffocation with a plastic bag, or beatings with electric cords were used. To save on bullets, throats were slit, heads were bashed with a shovel, or necks were broken with a hoe.

Babies were killed by dropping them from balconies or swinging them by their legs and smashing their heads against trees.[12]

When the Khmer Rouge was overthrown by a cadre of Cambodians backed by the Vietnamese in 1979, troops found fourteen bloated bodies, sticky pools of blood, and torture instruments at S-21. Duch didn't have time to destroy the records before he fled, which brought condemnation from his superiors. He disappeared and presumably was dead.

During its reign of terror, more than 14,000 prisoners entered S-21. Only seven are known to have survived. LaPel's cousin and her boyfriend were among those buried in shallow graves nearby.

"I weep when I think of what happened to her," LaPel said. "S-21 is now a genocide museum. Her youngest brother took me there in 1993. There are hundreds of mug shots of prisoners on the walls."

He blinked away tears. "We found the picture of my cousin."

His body language was clear. He didn't want to say anything more about it.

A Life Transformed

In 1994, fifteen years after the demise of the Pol Pot regime, LaPel and a team from his congregation bought farmland and built a church in the Battambang Province in northwestern Cambodia. The following year, he returned for two weeks to conduct leadership training among a hundred local Christians.

One of his key leaders invited a friend, Hang Pin, who was a teacher in a village not far away. Hang was in his mid-fifties and scrawny; his most distinguishing physical characteristic were his ears that stuck out. He spoke Thai and some English and had taught the Khmer language for a while at the Foreign Languages Institute in Beijing, China.

Although he wasn't a Christian, Hang agreed to attend LaPel's training because he was suffering from deepening depression and was looking for encouragement. Invaders had broken into his house and ordered his family on the floor. His wife, Rom, was bayoneted to death and Hang was stabbed in the back—a traditional Khmer Rouge punishment for betrayal.[13] He recovered, sold everything he owned, and moved to teach at a college in the Svay Chek district.

"He was shy, quiet, very withdrawn and discouraged, sitting in the back," LaPel recalled.

Typically, LaPel would end his sessions with an altar call, asking those who wanted to receive the forgiveness and leadership of Christ to come forward. Most in attendance were already followers of Jesus, and so, generally only a few responded. At the end of one class, LaPel was surprised to see that Hang had joined several others in stepping forward.

"I said to him, 'I'd like to pray for you. Do you have anything to say?'" LaPel told me.

"What did he tell you?"

"He said he had done a lot of bad things in his life. He said, 'I don't know if my brothers and sisters can forgive the sins I've committed.' He was sorry, he was remorseful."

"Did you ask for any details?"

"No, I was more concerned about the present: was he repentant, did he understand forgiveness is a gift of God's grace? And, yes, he did. I told him, 'God loves you. He can forgive you.' I prayed with him and the next day I baptized him in the Sangke River—and rarely have I seen such an immediate transformation in anyone."

"Really? How so?"

"His attitude, his demeanor—everything changed. Now he was sitting in the front row. He was dressed more neatly, he was excited, he would ask questions and interact with enthusiasm. He couldn't get enough teaching. He was the most attentive of all the students. He took meticulous notes and read the Bible eagerly. He couldn't wait to start a church in his village."

Before long, Hang received his certificate for completing the training. "I remember when we took our group picture," said LaPel. "He was standing right next to me in the front row. I put my hand on his shoulder."

Later LaPel got the word that Hang had returned to his village and led his children to Christ; then he baptized them. "After that he planted a house church," LaPel said. "Soon there were fourteen families. We continued to be in contact, and he came back for more leadership training."

Two years later, uprooted by military violence in his area, Hang ended up in Ban Ma Muang, a camp with 12,000 refugees inside Thailand. He began to serve with the American Refugee Committee (ARC), training health workers and saving countless lives by helping stem a typhoid outbreak.[14]

An ARC official called him "our best worker, highly respected in the community, clearly very intelligent and dedicated to helping the refugees." A journalist described him as a humanitarian.[15]

When the violence subsided in Cambodia, Hang returned and worked closely with World Vision, the Christian aid ministry, to provide healthcare to women and children. A World Vision leader called him "genuinely popular with the people."[16]

Over time, LaPel and Hang lost track of each other. That is, until a phone call woke up LaPel in his Los Angeles home in April 1999.

The Call That Changed Everything

The caller identified himself as a reporter for the Associated Press. "Could you help us identify one of your disciples?" he asked.

"One of my disciples?" replied LaPel. "Many people have come through my training."

The reporter described this individual—not very tall, skinny, his ears sticking out.

"Yes, I know him," said LaPel. "Hang Pin. He's one of our lay pastors."

"Well, he's hardline Khmer Rouge," said the reporter.

LaPel's mouth dropped open. "What do you mean?"

"He was one of the top Khmer Rouge. He's a killer. A mass murderer. He was in charge of S-21. Hang Pin is Comrade Duch!"

LaPel fell to his knees and slapped his forehead. His mind raced from his murdered cousin to the S-21 museum to baptizing Hang Pin. *Is this possible? How can this be?*

Slowly, the story emerged. Photojournalist Nic Dunlop had tracked down Duch in his jungle village, and then he and investigative reporter Nate Thayer, who had previously questioned Pol Pot, confronted Duch about his identity.[17]

At first, Duch was evasive. But then quickly he began admitting his past. "It is God's will you are here," Duch said to them. "Now my future is in God's hands. I have done very bad things in my life. Now it is time for *les represailles* [to bear the consequences] of my actions."

Dunlop and Thayer showed Duch copies of the documents he had signed to authorize executions. Even for a jaded foreign correspondent like Thayer, it seemed that Duch was genuinely remorseful.

"I am so sorry. The people who died were good people," Duch said, tears in his eyes. "The first half of my life I thought God was very bad, that only bad men prayed to God. My fault is that I didn't serve God, I served men, I served Communism. I feel very sorry about the killings and the past—I wanted to be a good Communist."

Now, he said, he had a new goal: "I want to tell everyone about the gospel."

Duch readily confessed to his crimes and said he would testify against other Khmer Rouge officials so that they too could be brought to justice. Anticipating his own arrest and imprisonment, Duch said,

"It is okay. They have my body. Jesus has my soul. It is important that this history be understood. I want to tell you everything clearly."

And, said Thayer, "He did."

Duch gave himself to authorities and eventually was put on trial before a United Nations–backed tribunal for crimes against humanity, murder, and torture. He didn't hide from his past as other Khmer Rouge killers were trying to do.

His testimony made headlines around the world because of his clear-cut confession of his offenses. "I am responsible for the crimes committed at S-21, especially the torture and execution of the people there," he told the five-judge international panel. "May I be permitted to apologize to the survivors of the regime and families of the victims who had loved ones who died brutally at S-21?"[18]

At one point, with his consent, Duch was taken in handcuffs back to blood-splattered S-21 to face his accusers. He collapsed in tears, saying, "I ask for your forgiveness—I know that you cannot forgive me, but I ask you to leave me the hope that you might."

Exclaimed one of the few S-21 survivors: "Here are the words that I have longed to hear for thirty years!"[19]

Convicted of his crimes, Duch today is locked in a prison in Phnom Penh for the rest of his life. The ruling is final.

The judicial system allows no appeal.

A True Conversion?

Christopher LaPel and the lay pastor he knew as Hang Pin, now unmasked as the infamous Duch, finally came face-to-face in 2008, after Duch had already spent nine years in military detention awaiting trial. A lawyer for the international tribunal had arranged the encounter at Duch's prison in Phnom Penh.

I tried to put myself in LaPel's position. *What would I say to Duch? What words would suffice? How would I act toward him?*

"What was the very first thing you said to him?" I asked LaPel.

"I said, 'Before we start, I want to tell you that I love you as my brother in Christ. I forgive you for what you've done to my family.'"

"It was as easy as that?" I asked, snapping my fingers.

He shook his head. "No, not easy — necessary. I had a long time to think and pray about this beforehand. How could I receive forgiveness from Christ for my sins but at the same time refuse to forgive someone for their sins — no matter how egregious?"

"How did he respond?"

"In his eyes I saw tears. As for me, I felt joy and peace in that moment. I felt liberated."

"What happened then?"

"We prayed together, and after that we praised God and I served him Communion. I read the Bible out loud, from the Twenty-Third Psalm."

The familiar passage came to my mind: "The LORD is my shepherd, I lack nothing.... You prepare a table before me in the presence of my enemies...."

I asked, "Did you talk about what happened at S-21?"

"No, I'm his pastor, not his prosecutor. Duch told me, 'The Holy Spirit has convicted my heart. I have to tell the world what I've done to my people. I will tell the truth, and the truth will set me free.'"

Since then, whenever LaPel makes one of his journeys to Cambodia, he goes to the prison to meet with Duch. His judicial pass, granted because of his status as a pastor, qualifies him as one of the few visitors allowed to see the inmate. He has brought him Cambodian Bibles, one in big print; a book of worship songs; and a Communion set. Each Sunday, as part of his own private worship session in a prison devoid of other Christians, Duch serves himself Communion in his sparsely furnished room.

"Since his conviction and sentence to life in prison, what is his demeanor?" I asked.

"When he sees me, he runs up to me, tears in his eyes. He is joyful, he is peaceful. Yes, he carries the weight of his crimes, but he is so thankful for God's grace. He is sharing Jesus with the guards and the other prisoners, who are former Khmer Rouge. He tells them there's forgiveness available for them as well."

"What does he say to you?"

"He told me, 'I'm not a prisoner; I'm a free man. I rejoice every day of my life. I deserve death. I deserve this punishment. But I have Jesus, and so I have love. If I had Jesus before, I never would have done what I did. I never knew about his love.'"

LaPel was called to testify at Duch's trial. The panel, which included three judges from Cambodia and one each from France and New Zealand, seemed fascinated by LaPel's description of Duch's spiritual metamorphosis.

The pastor described how Duch had admitted he was a sinner, received Christ as Lord and Savior, and was baptized. He talked about the Christian concepts of forgiveness, grace, and conversion. He discussed the value of reconciliation.

"For ninety minutes," LaPel told me, "they allowed me to preach the Good News."

At one point, a judge leaned forward and asked the question on everyone's mind: "Was this a true conversion?"

LaPel had sworn on the Bible to tell the truth.

He replied simply: "Yes."

Breaking the Cycle

Theravada Buddhism is, by far, the dominant religion in Cambodia, practiced by nine out of ten people and woven deeply into the fabric of Cambodian culture.[20] Duch's fate would be clear under Buddhist theology—his grievous sins would follow him as bad karma, which he would have to try to work off over many successive lifetimes.

In fact, when journalist Mary Murphy traveled to Cambodia in 2008 to pursue the Duch story, she met some Buddhist monks who scoffed at the news of Duch's conversion.

"Duch has become a Christian to earn points," one insisted, predicting Duch would return in the next life in a form reflecting the depth of his depravity. Asked what form, he replied: "A bug."[21]

I recounted that anecdote to LaPel. "To a lot of people," I said, "that would seem to be a better picture of justice, given the brutality of Duch's crimes."

"Justice, maybe. But grace is not fair. And everyone should be grateful for that, not just Duch. If God were to deny Duch grace by drawing a line and saying, 'No more,' then who's to say where the line might be drawn next time?

"Jesus's death has infinite value because he's an infinite God; it was enough to cover all the sins of the world. If we say some sin is too terrible, then we're saying Jesus fell short in his mission. Grace is only grace if it's available even to the Duchs of the world. In fact," he said, straightening himself in his chair, "here's a difficult thing for us to comprehend: God loves Duch as much as he loves you and me."

I allowed myself to feel the full impact of that statement. "That *is* hard to accept," I said.

LaPel continued, "The truth is that God looked beneath the filth that covered Duch's life and saw a core that is made in his image. That image is obscured but never destroyed. When the Bible says God loves the world, it doesn't footnote any exceptions. God's grace is inexhaustible.

"Perhaps we don't think we need as much grace as Duch does, because, after all, our sins aren't as egregious. We conveniently forget our various forms of idolatry, our blasphemy, our daily transgressions of God's teachings. No, we don't deserve grace — and neither does Duch. For each of us, it is a gift."

"Still," I said to LaPel, "should saying a simple prayer be sufficient to erase the penalty for so many awful crimes?"

"Simple prayer—no, it's more than that. When we authentically come to God in repentance and faith, when we confess our sins and turn from them, he has promised to forgive us. Now, it's also true that Duch will suffer the justice of this world; he will never walk the street again. Even though God has forgiven him, he will always carry remorse for his crimes."

His comment reminded me of a conversation I once had with Christian philosopher Ravi Zacharias, who might as well have been describing Duch when he said, "The more he is in tune with who Christ is, the deeper will be his pain for what he has done."[22]

Yet Duch's victims are buried in mass graves in the Killing Fields of Choeung Ek, while Duch is slowly gaining weight on three meals a day in prison. Often our demand for retribution chafes against the generosity of grace.

"If Jesus is the only way to salvation," I said, "then the irony is that his Buddhist victims would go to hell, but Duch would spend eternity in heaven."

LaPel stroked his chin. "Yes, I believe Jesus is the only way to heaven; that's why I spend my life telling people about him," he replied. "None of us is truly innocent; we've all sinned, and the only way a person can have confidence of their salvation is by receiving forgiveness through Christ. Thankfully, that forgiveness is available to everyone who is willing to receive it.

"But how much does someone have to know to be saved?" he asked. "If a person calls out to God for mercy in the moments before death, does God hear him? If they reach out to the one true God as best they know how, will he answer? Nobody is saved apart from Christ's work on the cross, but only God knows how much a person must understand in order to adequately respond. The Bible assures us that ultimately God will do what is right.[23] And I have the utmost confidence in that."

I asked him what the rest of Cambodia thinks. Do they agree with that monk's comment, or do they believe that even Duch could be redeemed?

"Many are hearing of his strong faith and saying, 'Look how God can change a life,'" LaPel said. "They are surprised he would admit his guilt and humbly ask forgiveness. They're saying, 'Look at these Christians—they are forgiving. Why can't we do that too?' I think, in the end, this will help the churches in Cambodia. God is opening up hearts and minds to see that Jesus is love and that he can bring healing and hope.

"That's very important," he continued, "because grace is unknown in Buddhism. So many Cambodians hold in their hatred and anger; they don't know how to release it. Someday, it might erupt into another era of violence. Maybe if Cambodians can learn about forgiveness through the story of Duch, it can break the cycle. What else but grace can do that?

"Wouldn't it be just like God," he said, "to turn the Killing Fields into the Harvest Fields?"

CHAPTER 6

The Homeless

A Gesture of Grace Can Change a Life

Grace means there is nothing we can do to make
God love us more ... and there is nothing we can do
to make God love us less.

Philip Yancey[1]

He was digging in a dumpster behind a pizzeria in Las Vegas, hunting for half-eaten chicken wings and scraps of crust, when suddenly the hopelessness of his situation hit him with full force.

It's come to this—I'm eating out of garbage cans. I'm sleeping in the dirt. I'm filthy and I stink and I'm starving to death. And there's no way out. Oh God, there's no future and no hope. Why are you doing this to me? He collapsed in the trash and began to sob. The tears wouldn't stop.

"If I had owned a gun, I would have put it in my mouth and pulled the trigger," Cody Huff was saying to me. "I swear to you, I would have. I'd lost everything, I was an addict, I'd been in and out of jail, I was homeless, I was shunned, every last ounce of my dignity was gone. I hated myself, I hated my life—and I hated God."

Now, tears pooled once more. "That was the day I hit bottom. I couldn't go any lower." He dug into his back pocket for a handkerchief. "I was so hungry, I was so exhausted, I was so desperate, I was so ashamed. I had nothing left. Do you know what that feels like? I *had* nothing and I *was* nothing."

Cody was headed, inexorably, toward destruction. He had been a burglar, a drug dealer, a counterfeiter, and a scammer. He had been beaten, shot at, and stabbed. He had sat atop mountains of cash and frittered it all away on meth and heroin.

His life was in a tailspin — and then it all came down to one moment. No, not *that* moment — not the time he was crying bitterly in the garbage. That seemed like the end, only it turned out it wasn't.

There was a brief, unlikely, spontaneous experience of grace yet to come — and with it, an insight for me on how to bring grace to others.

Gladiator School

With bristly gray hair, a goatee, and arms decorated with tattoos, Cody was sitting across from me in an armless upholstered chair. His face was weathered, his voice raspy at times — the effects of being kicked in the throat after being jumped by a gang years ago. He looked every bit of his sixty years — and more. And yet his tone was humble and his spirit meek as he talked with painful candor about a life that was one long and frightening slide toward hell.

"My dad? No, I never knew my father. He was nineteen when he got my mom pregnant. She was fourteen. They were forced into getting married, and then he took off," Cody said.

"Did you ever connect with him?" I asked, my pen poised above a legal pad.

"Many years later, I called him and asked if he ever wondered what had become of me," Cody replied. "He told me, 'No, not really.'"

Cody's mother dropped out of school and worked as a waitress and then a bank teller in a small town north of Sacramento. Cody doesn't like to discuss the physical abuse he endured — only that life was chaotic and traumatic, leading him to start smoking marijuana as a way of escape when he was twelve years old. The following year, he fled to live in a hippie commune in an old Victorian house in San Francisco.

"There I was — thirteen years old, selling an underground newspaper on the streets and chipping in money for food and drugs. Anywhere from fourteen to eighteen people lived in the house. We had the *real* stuff—orange sunshine LSD-25, magic mushrooms, mescaline. I've probably taken LSD two hundred times in my life."

The authorities found him four months later, leading to his first stint in juvenile hall. Only a short time after he got out, he was arrested for his first felony—a hit-and-run car accident—and sent to the California Youth Authority. Essentially, it was a prison for kids. He was fifteen.

"We had a name for it—Gladiator School, because, in effect, they would give you a garbage can lid and a shank and you're on your own," he said. "I learned how to fight, how to make drugs, how to sell drugs —it was an education in running a criminal enterprise. I was a fast learner. And when I got out a year later, I started putting all of that education to work."

From Jail to Nursing to Vegas

It didn't take long for Cody to become a thriving businessman—in the illicit drug trade.

"I had great products—cocaine, psychedelics, marijuana—and I offered excellent customer service. I even had a pipeline for selling drugs to the inmates at Soledad Prison. Pretty soon, I was making thousands of dollars a week and living on the beach near Monterey. It was all parties and rock concerts. I was buying whatever I wanted, whenever I wanted. And then I did something incredibly stupid. I put a needle in my arm."

"Heroin?"

"Yeah. Within six months I was going through ten bags a day. You get to the point with heroin that you don't care if you eat or if you have a place to sleep—all you care about is getting a hit. I began to sell off everything just to buy the drug. Before long I had lost it all, so I started committing robberies and thefts. We would work with prostitutes by posing as cops and busting in to rob their clients. Once we got a master key to a hotel and stole forty color-television sets. When they came to arrest me, I had a hypodermic needle and some heroin in my back pocket. They gave me a year in jail."

At least, I thought to myself, this forced him to go through detox. "Did you come out clean?"

"Yeah, I did. It became very clear that half of Monterey was wanting to kill me for the stuff I'd done, so I left with just a few pieces of clothing and headed for San Diego."

"You decided to go straight?"

"Uh, no. I started committing home burglaries. Again, I was pretty successful—I went two years without getting caught. I used drugs casually—no heroin—and I only had to break into a house once a week or even once a month, the money was that good. But it all ended when someone saw me go through the window of a place on the beach and called the police. When I came out, they arrested me. With my prior record, the judge gave me one to fifteen years in prison."

"What were you thinking when the judge imposed the sentence?"

Cody pursed his lips. "I wasn't thinking about the one year; I was fixated on the fifteen. I thought, *I'm going to be forty by the time I get out. I'll be an old man!* The next morning, I was handcuffed, shackled, and taken by prison bus to the California State Prison in Chino. I was still a kid. I'd been to juvenile hall and jails—but prison? This was the scariest place I'd ever seen. Fortunately, I got through it all right, because my underworld connections gave me protection."

Released after a year, he returned to San Diego and moved in with a woman who worked as a private nurse. "Cody, why don't you go to nursing school?" she suggested one day. Amazingly, he agreed, and this high school dropout and convicted felon managed to become a Licensed Practical Nurse.

Somehow he was hired at a prestigious hospital that didn't bother to run a background check—and from then on, future employers never questioned his résumé. That credential was a golden ticket.

For four years, he worked legitimate jobs as a nurse. But then he and his girlfriend broke up. "Whenever I got emotionally upset, I went back to my old friend—heroin," he said. "I went off the deep end. I was desperate to get a new start, so I went to a fresh place— Las Vegas."

"Vegas? Seriously?"

"Yeah, that was another stupid decision," he said. "If you're trying to get off drugs and away from partying, that's the last place in the world you want to go."

"Tell me about your first day there."

"I sat down in a bar. A guy drinking a beer said, 'What are you doing in Vegas?' He looked cool, so I said, 'I've been doing too many drugs and to tell you the truth, I'm feeling sick right now.' He said, 'Do you want to get well?' I said, 'Do you know somebody?' He said, '*Know* somebody? I *am* somebody!'

"We walked two blocks away, and he sold me heroin—and that started me on another slide that went real bad, real quick. I started doing drugs, partying, spending my savings from nursing like it was going out of style. After three months, I was running low on cash."

That's when Cody learned how to really make money—literally. "I got into a counterfeiting ring," he explained. "We were making silver dollars out of lead—no kidding, you couldn't tell them from the real thing. We would make a thousand of them and use them in slot machines. We were trading our phony money for their real money —and then we'd buy drugs. Above all else, I had to feed my habit."

After two years, the FBI, the police, and Nevada gaming authorities began pursuing Cody. They posted his picture all over the city. Figuring it was only a matter of time until they arrested him, Cody turned himself in. He was sentenced to another year in jail.

Cody sighed. "It was just endless," he said. "I would gain everything, then lose it all. I'd get off drugs, then I'd get hooked again. I'd work a legitimate job as a nurse, then I'd get back into crime. In all, I've done eight years in prison. That's a long time behind bars, Lee —*eight years*. That does something to your heart. It becomes tough as leather."

How to Be Homeless

Out of jail once more, Cody was approached to provide in-home nursing care for an eighty-year-old woman in exchange for room and board. Fed up with how his life was going, he recognized this as a chance to go straight. Soon he was cooking her meals, cleaning her house, mowing her lawn, and taking her to doctor appointments. He was off drugs, and she began paying him a salary.

"Over time, this woman became like a grandmother to me," he said. "You see, I never had a family. I never knew what it was like to have someone just love you. I told her everything about my past and said, 'So, Mimi, this is what you're dealing with.' Mimi, it turned out, was a Christian, and she said, 'You know what? God forgives you and I forgive you.'"

The more Mimi encouraged him, the more he wanted to serve her. He was her caretaker and surrogate grandson at the same time. On his days off, Cody turned his love of fishing into a lucrative sideline, winning professional bass tournaments and amassing a bulging bank account. His life seemed to be healthy for the first time—until Mimi developed organic brain syndrome and rapidly began to deteriorate.

"I loved Mimi, and I had to watch her lose her mind. It broke my heart. I couldn't take it. I knew I should have been stronger, but I never loved a patient like that and didn't know what to do.

"One day I was at a friend's house, and he lit up a pipe to smoke crack. I said, 'Give me a hit.' He looked at me and said, 'Cody, you

CHAPTER 6: *The Homeless*   113

don't want a hit of this.' I said, 'Yeah, I do.' Before long, I was smoking a thousand dollars of crack a night. It was worse than heroin. Then Mimi died, and I really went off the deep end. I didn't care about anything. It was all about girls and crack, that's all."

Within eighteen months, Cody burned through all his savings. He was kicked out of his house—and that began nearly a year of homelessness on the gritty streets of Las Vegas, far from the glittery lights of the Strip.

"I had nowhere to go, I had no money, I had a drug habit, I didn't know what to do," he recalled. "I didn't even know how to be home-less. I filled a backpack with some jeans, T-shirts, sweatshirts, a few pairs of socks, some toothpaste, and a toothbrush. I didn't even think to take a sleeping bag.

"The first day I went around and interviewed homeless people. I'd say, 'My name is Cody, and I've never been homeless. Could I ask you a few questions? Like, where do you clean up? Where do you go to the bathroom? Where's the best part of town to be? How do you eat?'

"I slept in a dirt field that first night, and when I woke up I was really hungry. I walked up to a man and said, 'Sir, could you spare a couple of bucks so I could get a hamburger? I haven't eaten since yesterday.' And with that, I just burst into tears. He told me, 'Go get a job!' and I started cussing at him.

"I couldn't bring myself to beg anymore. It was so demeaning. So I hustled a couple of bucks and bought a bottle of window cleaner. As people drove into a shopping center, I'd say, 'Could I clean the windows of your car for you?' They'd ask, 'What do you charge?' I'd say, 'Just make a donation.' That's how I took care of myself when I was homeless."

"What was your day like?"

"I would work full bore, night and day, for three straight days, without a break. By then I'd have forty or fifty dollars in my pocket.

I'd take a bus to Fremont Street, where all the crack dealers were, and I'd buy fifty bucks worth of crack."

"How long did it take to smoke it?"

He shrugged. "Ten minutes."

"Then what?"

"I'd get back on the bus, go to another shopping center and work again for three days straight. By then, I was exhausted. I'd fall asleep in a park. Flies were all over me; it didn't matter. Every once in a while, a Catholic priest would bring sandwiches to the homeless there. At eleven in the evening, when the park closed, all the homeless would go over to a dirt field behind the police department. I had blankets and quilts that I'd find in garbage cans."

Before long, he hit bottom. That's when he was scrounging around in the dumpster behind the pizzeria, scavenging for anything edible, and he was overcome with desperation. There seemed to be no path out.

"I sat there and just cried and cried. It was bad enough being homeless, but you lose your self-respect and self-esteem little by little. The world makes you feel like you don't matter. You just want to die."

"They Don't Care"

"Were there times when you tried to get assistance?" I asked.

"Yeah, once I went to the mental-health department and said, 'I'm crazy. I need help.' They said, 'We can't do anything for you. You're a dope addict. Get out of here!'

"And I tried to look for a job. I'd shave, I'd get a clean T-shirt, I'd go to the bathroom in the park and try to bathe. They had a nozzle where you could get water for your dog, and I'd use that to shampoo my hair. But I still looked horrible.

"I'd walk into a business and say, 'I'm going to be real honest with you—I'm homeless. I can't even feed myself. I'll do anything—I'll paint, clean, do your dishes, wash your car, pull weeds.' And they'd say, 'You've gotta be kidding! Get outta here before I call the police!'

"It got to the point in the last four or five months of being homeless that I just didn't care anymore. It didn't matter to me if my teeth fell out or if I smelled. I dropped to 135 pounds. If I took off my shirt, you could count my ribs. I wore pants with a thirty-inch waist, and I had to take a shoestring and tie the loops together just to get them to stay up. I was getting busted pretty regularly for jaywalking, vagrancy, smoking crack in public, trespassing."

"How did people treat you?"

"Horribly. If I was walking across the street, some cars would speed up, like they were trying to hit me."

"Seriously?"

"Yeah. You know the old saying, 'You treat me like a dog?' Man, you know what? Dogs are treated a whole lot better than homeless people. I remember how it feels when people don't really care if you lie down and die. Honestly, they don't care."

I was feeling guilty about my attitude toward homeless people I had encountered through the years.

"What was it like at night?" I asked.

"Bone-chilling in the winters. It wouldn't snow, but sometimes there was a cold rain. I'd pick a blanket out of the garbage and a piece of plastic that painters use. When it would rain, I'd use those to try to keep myself and my stuff dry. Sometimes when it rained I'd go down to a homeless shelter, but really, they didn't treat us much better. In the summertime, it gets oppressively hot, over a hundred degrees, and at night I would just swelter. There was no relief."

"Did you find some generous people?"

"Every once in a while. I remember being in a grocery-store parking lot and a woman in a red car drove in. I don't have anything wrong with my leg, but when I was washing car windows I limped. So I limped up to the car and said, 'Excuse me, ma'am, could I clean your windows?' She said, 'Well, I just got my car detailed, so I don't need that. But are you hungry?' I said, 'I'm starving.'

"She reached into her purse and pulled out a five-dollar gift certificate from a hamburger place. It was a life-saver. I went and had a couple of hamburgers, French fries, a soft drink—I spent all but twelve cents of that certificate. Man, that felt good.

"After months without a shower, wearing the same clothes day after day, I began to smell terrible. When I'd come back to the field at night, I reeked so bad that the other homeless could smell me thirty feet away. They started yelling at me. 'Cody, you stink!' 'Cody, get some clean clothes!' 'Cody, you need a bath!'

"Finally, the guy next to me told me about Central Christian Church."

That name sounded familiar. "That's where Jud Wilhite is the pastor," I said.

"That's right. They would let the homeless come and take a shower, shave, get clean clothes, have breakfast, and go to a service if they wanted. That sounded good to me—all except for the service—so I said I'd go with that guy the next day, which was Sunday. We got up at four in the morning and walked seven miles to get there."

"Was it worth it for the meal and clothes?"

He chuckled. "Oh, it was worth it, all right, but not just for those things," he said. "You see, this was the day that changed my life."

A Gesture of Grace

Cody was waiting upstairs at Central Christian, the gleaming megachurch in the suburb of Henderson, clutching a number that secured his place in line for a shower. Several homeless men were milling around, so he didn't feel conspicuous. Tables offered free coffee and food.

That's when, unnoticed by Cody, a volunteer named Michelle

came in. Middle-aged and petite, Michelle surveyed the room, then walked over to him and said, "Sir?"

Cody turned and found Michelle looking him straight in the eyes. "Sir," she said simply, "You look like you need a hug."

Cody was aghast. *A hug?* He was gaunt, his hair matted, his beard scraggly, his clothes dirty and stained, his teeth rotting in his mouth. *A hug?* He shook his head. "Ma'am, I haven't taken a shower in three months," he said. "I smell horrible."

Michelle smiled. "You don't smell to me," she said—and then she wrapped her arms around him. Again, she looked him in the eyes. "Do you know," she said, "that Jesus loves you?"

Jesus can't love me, Cody was thinking. *I'm homeless. Jesus can't love me. I'm a drug addict. I'm a bad man.*

"Jesus loves you," she repeated.

What can God accomplish through the simple gesture of a hug? Are three words about Jesus sufficient to redeem a lost soul? How much can one expression of love straighten a path that has been crooked from the start?

At that moment, in an instant, something spiritual sparked inside of Cody Huff. To this day, years later, he can't talk about it without his voice cracking.

"Plain and simple, that was the pivotal moment of my life," he told me. "It was like a personal encounter with Jesus. It was love—pure love. She didn't care what I looked like or how much I smelled. It was like Jesus himself was standing in front of me and saying, 'Cody, I love you.'

"At the time in my life when I was the least lovable, when everyone shunned me, when there was no hope of getting out of the mess I was in, when I smelled so bad that even the other homeless didn't want to be around me—there she was, with this simple expression of the grace of God. And something happened in my heart."

"What was it?"

Cody glanced off to the side, gathering his thoughts, then looked back at me. He started to say something but stopped. Then he said, "Honestly, Lee, I don't know. All I can say is that it was a spiritual moment. It was a hug, but it was more than that—it was what the hug was saying to me: I accept you. I care about you. You matter to me. You have value and worth. You have dignity as a human being.

"That was the first time in so long that anyone cared if I lived or died. Even I didn't care anymore. I think that's why I kept doing the drugs; I was hoping that the next hit would stop my heart.

"And then," he said, "this hug." He snapped his fingers. "It changed everything."

A Prayer in the Dirt

Cody got his shower that day at Central Christian, put on some clean clothes, ate a good breakfast, and then sat in on a Bible study.

"Right away something was different," he told me. "It was like a light switch had been turned on. The more I heard about Jesus, the more I wanted to hear. Then Michelle said, 'Do you want to go to church?' I said, 'Well, yeah, but the building might fall down!'

"We went to the service, and I sat in the highest row, way up in the balcony, in the dark, where nobody could see me. The pastor, Jud, got up and said some older ladies had been complaining that the music the kids were playing in church was too loud. 'I'm going to tell you how I feel about this,' Jud said. 'If those kids are playing music and worshiping Jesus—I say turn it up!' And I thought, *Yes, this is my kind of church!*"

Starting that day, Cody's appetite for Jesus was insatiable. He trudged back and forth to the church. He started cutting back on the drugs. He attended the church's ministry for the homeless. Everything culminated three weeks later in the park that he called home.

"I didn't really know anything about the Bible, except God loves me, Jesus died for me, I'm a sinner, forgiveness is available — and I wanted it," he told me.

"I didn't even know how to pray. I got on my knees, with my face in the dirt, crying like a baby, and I just poured out my heart. I said, 'God, I'm so tired. I'm tired of the drugs. Please, take them away from me. It's like I've been driving my own car and all I do is get into head-on crashes. Why don't you drive? I'm sorry for the way I've lived. I want to surrender my life to you. God, please make me a new man.'

"I can't even tell you how long I prayed — maybe ten or fifteen minutes — and when I said, 'Amen,' I was consumed by the most incredible peace I'd ever felt. It was like a wave in the ocean, like when I was surfing and a wave would *whoosh* over me. I felt clean for the first time. I didn't know where all this was leading, but starting right then, God took away my desire for drugs."

"That doesn't happen for everyone," I said.

"I know. It can be a process and a struggle. But for me, everything began to change right away. In fact, that evening, there were about forty of us sleeping in that field. Before then, nobody had ever offered me drugs for free. That night, they kept waking me and offering me crack pipes. My best friend said, 'Here, Cody, I just put ten dollars on this.' I said, 'Steve, get away from me. I quit. I'm done. Dude, I've turned over my life to Jesus Christ.' He said, 'What do you mean, Cody?' I said, 'I don't know what it all looks like, but I'm his now. I don't do that stuff anymore.'

"Three weeks later, I got baptized. I was scared to death in front of all those people, but Michelle was there. She said, 'Cody, ain't nothing can keep me away from seeing you baptized.'

"I kept going to the Bible study every week and church every week. I couldn't get enough of the Bible. I started telling everyone about Jesus, even though I didn't really know that much about him. I'd be holding little Scripture studies in the field, using a pocket Bible."

Cody became a volunteer at the church. The cook would make

him enormous sandwiches for lunch. "I can't eat all this," Cody would say. The cook would hand him some plastic wrap. "Then you've got dinner for later," he replied. Pretty soon, through a connection at the church, Cody was offered a job and a place to live. For the first time in years, he was gainfully employed and self-supporting.

He kept serving in the church's homeless ministry. Once they were providing food to a group of homeless people who lived under a bridge, and Cody saw another volunteer who looked familiar. He had seen that face somewhere before. *Where was it?* Oh, yeah, she was the woman in the red car who had given him the food certificate when he was homeless.

He introduced himself and told her his story. "I'm sorry—I give out so many of those coupons that I don't remember you," she said. "But I'm thrilled you're a Christian now!"

She's a nice lady, thought Cody. Her name was Heather.

New Life in the Park

Eight years later, on a balmy spring evening during a trip to Las Vegas, I was watching as dozens of homeless men and women gathered under a big gazebo in Myron E. Leavitt Park, across the street from Jake's Bar. One disheveled man with a broken leg arrived in a shopping cart pushed by a friend. Smoke was rising from charcoal grills as chicken was barbecued for those who would show up.

Everyone's attention was riveted on the enthusiastic gray-haired man in a T-shirt and jeans, clutching a Bible in one hand and pointing off into the distance with the other.

"I used to sleep in the dirt not far from here," he was saying into a microphone. "Then a woman gave me a hug and told me that Jesus loves me. There she is, over there—sitting in the back. It was a moment of grace for me. And friends, I don't care what you've been through—Jesus will take you in his arms too. He will hug you like she hugged me. Only with Jesus, he will never let you go."

Cody Huff is an ordained minister now at Hope Church in Las Vegas, having been mentored by Pastor Vance Pittman. Cody works with boundless energy as the volunteer director of Broken Chains, a ministry that helps feed and house the homeless of Las Vegas.[2] It's supported by a number of churches and local businesses—including a retailer that used to call the cops on Cody when he was a vagrant in their parking lot. The city's mayor seeks Cody's advice about the poor. He gets invited to address training classes of police officers, like the ones who used to harass him when he would sleep in the park.

These days Cody holds regular events in that same park, where Broken Chains offers free meals, music, and spiritual encouragement. And the woman wielding the tongs as she grills the chicken? That's Heather, the one with the red car. She's Cody's wife now.

After Cody shared his story to the crowd that evening, the home-less lined up so Heather could serve them dinner. Later I found myself standing among the picnic tables and chatting with Cody, who was watching with satisfaction as his guests devoured their food.

He chuckled. "You know, when I prayed to Jesus on my knees in the dirt, I told him I'd follow him even if he wanted me to stay in this park the rest of my life," Cody told me. "Little did I know, that was his plan."

These are his people, this congregation of misfits, crack addicts, and drunks, the unshaven, unwashed, unemployed, and unwanted. I think that night Cody must have hugged them all.

I strolled over to Michelle, who was wearing a necklace with a small silver cross. She was standing in the back, taking everything in.

"Did you think when you gave Cody a hug that it would lead to all this?" I asked.

Her smile was modest. "No, who could have foreseen this?"

"Why did you do it?" I asked. "When Cody was dirty and smelly and homeless—why did you offer him a hug?"

She looked at me like it was the stupidest question ever—and maybe it was. "Because he looked like he needed one," she replied. "That's what Jesus would do, isn't it?"

No doubt that's true. But what about me? Back on that day, would I have shaken Cody's hand or given him a bear hug or even a pat on the back? Would I have gone out of my way to tell him about Jesus? Would I have seen the potential for redemption and transformation? Would I have given him the dignity he deserved?

I pondered those questions for a while, and I winced at my answers. How many times have I encountered someone like Cody on the street and thought of him more as a problem to be solved than a person to be loved? How often have I hoarded grace?

I said good-bye to Michelle and scanned the crowd under the gazebo. I decided to walk over to the scruffy young man who had arrived in a shopping cart, his leg in a cast. He was sitting by himself on the periphery.

"My name's Lee," I said. "What's yours?"

His eyelids were drooping. "They call me Spider." His voice was hoarse.

Hesitantly, I draped my arm around his shoulder. "Well, Spider, tell me your story," I said. "And then let me tell you about a friend who has changed my life. His name is Jesus—and he loves you."

CHAPTER 7

The Pastor

*Can We Forgive the Most Personal of Wounds—
And Ourselves?*

> *To live by grace means to acknowledge my whole life story, the
> light side and the dark. In admitting my shadow side I learn
> who I am and what God's grace means.*
>
> Brennan Manning[1]

He was a seminary graduate, the former leader of a prayer ministry, a popular speaker, the husband of his childhood sweetheart, a father of three, the senior pastor of a thriving church—and my friend. Now there he was, standing alone on the stage, looking out at faces shrouded in darkness and announcing his resignation from the church he loved so much.

"I have broken the covenant of my marriage through adultery," he told the stunned congregation. "I have sinned against God, my family, and you. I have repented of my sin and seek your forgiveness. Jesus hasn't failed you, but I have."

Brad Mitchell walked off the stage, out the back door, and drove home to his wife, Heidi. Together, they cried until it was time to repeat his confession at the next service. By far, it was the lowest point of their lives.

Unfortunately, infidelity has become commonplace. In 41 percent of marriages, one or both spouses admit to physical or emotional cheating.[2] Newspaper headlines over the years have documented—with distressing regularity—the accounts of religious leaders whose marital betrayals have cost them their pulpits. Few of these stories, though, describe the pain, the struggle, the loss, and the humiliation that these preachers and their spouses invariably go through.

Grace? These pastors have spoken on the topic countless times. They've taught the story of the Prodigal Son, preached on the theology of the cross, described the Christian necessity of offering grace to each other, and served the bread and the wine that represent the price Jesus paid to open heaven's floodgates of forgiveness. But suddenly, mired in their own sin and shame, grace can seem so much more elusive to them.

Can a wife offer grace to a husband who has trashed their wedding vows and dishonored her in such a public way? And can the pastor, exposed as a hypocrite, finally come to the place of forgiving himself —perhaps the most difficult expression of grace there is?

Before we feel smug, this is more than a spectator sport for the rest of us. After all, don't each of us struggle with the same issues to some degree—forgiving those closest to us who have broken our hearts in one way or the other (in my case, my father), and finding ways to ease our own guilt when we have transgressed a moral boundary that we swore we would never breach? We want to throw stones at the Christian leaders who have let us down—but who among us can hurl the first rock?

Those thoughts coursed through my mind as I sat in the family room of my house with Brad and Heidi, who were next to each other on the couch. I have known Brad for more than twenty years. He had always been the straightest of arrows, the solid rock of faith, a passionate preacher of the Bible, the first to offer a prayer or encouragement to others, and the face of authenticity, integrity, and consistency.

Words like infidelity, disgrace, moral failure—no, they could never describe my friend. That was what made the news of his extramarital affair—and the resulting collapse of his life—so shocking.

Anybody but Brad, I remember thinking. Yet there we were: Brad and Heidi, at times tearful, candidly describing how his ministry and marriage went spiraling out of control and how he embarked on his personal quest for grace—from God, Heidi, and from himself.

They appear to be the ideal couple. Brad, with chiseled good looks, occasionally works as a model; Heidi, her blond hair cascading to her shoulders, is articulate and pretty.

It wasn't easy for them to reveal the private details of their lives, including his indiscretions that nearly shipwrecked their marriage. But they had agreed it would be worth their discomfort if it could help others.

Later I found out that when I briefly left the room after they had discussed some particularly painful events, Brad leaned over and whispered, "I'm so sorry." His tone said it all: *You never deserved any of this.* Replied Heidi: "It's in the past."

The journey to that moment, however, was long, arduous—and uncertain.

The Journey Together

The courtship of Brad and Heidi was anything but conventional. Brad was in the sixth grade when he first met the younger Heidi after a church service. He quickly coined a nickname for her: "Hideous Heidi."

As the best friend of Brad's sister, Heidi was constantly over at Brad's house during the two-and-a-half years he lived in North Dakota. He would harass and tease them mercilessly. When his family moved to Indianapolis, he promptly put her out of his mind.

Then Heidi came to Indiana to visit Brad's sister when Brad was sixteen years old. The girls were giggling in a bedroom as Brad arrived home from his job at a warehouse. He settled into a chair downstairs

to read the sports section. That's when Heidi, now fourteen years old
— fresh-faced and cute, her blond hair flowing — came sweeping
through the room.

"Hi, Brad," she said, almost off-handedly.

Brad glanced at her. The words that came out of his mouth were
nonchalant: "Hi, Heidi." But inside, he was reeling — *Oh my goodness!
Wow! What in the world happened to her?*

Smitten, he later invited her to look at his football photos. Before
she left his room, he kissed her. And before the end of the weekend, he
actually proposed to her — and she accepted. There they were, sixteen
and fourteen, too young for her father to let her date, and in their
minds they were future husband and wife.

Looking back, Brad said, "She was everything I wanted, so I figured, why not lock this up?"

Recalled Heidi: "I knew I wanted to get married someday, and
suddenly here was this perfect guy. He had morphed from a junior
high dweeb into a high school football player with sideburns and
everything. I thought, *This is great! We can be engaged, and my dad
doesn't have to know.*"

They worked out the details. They would date other people as they
got older, just to make sure they were right for each other. They would
go through the same Bible studies and write letters back and forth
about how they were growing spiritually. They would attend the same
Christian college. They would get married after his graduation, and he
would become an attorney or pursue some other lucrative profession.

Amazingly, just as they planned, everything came to pass — except
there was one development they hadn't foreseen. When Brad was tour-
ing Europe with a singing group from Wheaton College, he would
feel a tug from the Holy Spirit. As he looked at the majestic cathedrals
— ancient and beautiful sanctuaries that used to be teeming with wor-
shipers — he saw architectural grandeur but spiritual shells.

America is just a couple of generations away from the same thing, he thought to himself. *We can't let that happen. We've got to do everything we can to build God's church.*

The Rise to Success

After earning a master's of divinity degree and serving an extended internship, Brad was named senior pastor of a church in Minnesota. Well, it wasn't much of a congregation at the time—just six families. But over the next several years, thanks in part to Brad's engaging sermons and personable style, the church grew to more than four hundred.

"I loved seeing people fall in love with Jesus," he said. "It's exciting to see them enjoy his presence and grow in their faith." During his tenure, five hundred people trusted Christ through the ministries of the church.

His success opened the door to a position with a much higher profile: director of the men's sports and prayer ministries at one of America's largest and most innovative churches—a prestigious and challenging role in which Brad flourished. Now with three children, Brad and Heidi's marriage was good.

"I'd give it a B-plus," Heidi offered.

Brad nodded. "That's about right," he said. "We were happy, but I was traveling two or three weekends a month to speak somewhere, so that added stress. And our styles of dealing with conflict were different—she was a peacemaker, and I was a peacekeeper."

"What's the difference?"

"We were outspoken and competitive by nature," Heidi explained. "We'd have conflict, we'd debate and argue, and I saw that as a good thing. We'd work through the issue and come out better—or so I thought. I didn't hold grudges, and I didn't think he did either."

"On the other hand, I tried to avoid conflict," Brad added. "I'd try to keep the peace and end up stifling my emotions. I'd come across as if everything had been resolved, but I was masking and suppressing my anger—and then I would erupt over little things."

After a few years, Brad seized an opportunity to become senior pastor of a church in Michigan. Again, God seemed to bless his efforts. In a no-growth community, the church expanded from 1,800 people to almost 4,000 in six years. Baptisms shot up tenfold. Giving more than doubled in a stagnant economy. The number of people in small groups tripled.

Accolades came from the congregation, and yet there was tension between Brad and some of the church's leaders. The growth was creating organizational problems, and the culture of the formerly buttoned-down church was changing to reflect Brad's more informal and approachable style. For the first time, many spiritually wayward people were venturing into the church and finding Jesus. Brad was told to preach deeper messages to satisfy some of the church's leaders, while he was more focused on reaching newcomers and bringing them to faith in Christ.

"A lot of me wants to please people," said Brad, "and when some of the leaders weren't happy with me, and I didn't feel like they were validating or appreciating me—well, that was pride. 'Pride is the mother hen under which all other sins are hatched,' says C. S. Lewis. I became defensive and bitter. I wasn't trusting God's sovereignty. I felt I deserved better. I wanted to escape like Jonah and run away."

In a way, that's what he did. He jumped to a church in South Carolina. It was contemporary, casual, and had a thriving sports ministry, a great staff, and supportive leaders. In so many ways, it was a much better fit for him.

But in the midst of making that move—during a time when Heidi and Brad didn't realize the depth of his unhealthy thinking —they made a decision that planted the seeds of his downfall.

A Whiff of the Apple

At the time, the Michigan housing market was bleak. It would take a long time for Brad and Heidi to sell their home so they could move to South Carolina. Also, their daughter understandably wanted to complete her senior year in high school before the transition. So Brad and Heidi came up with a plan: he would move to the East Coast while she would stay in Michigan. He would fly home to visit for a week out of every month.

"We had seen this model used by another pastor," Brad said. "We figured we could put up with anything for a year."

Only, it didn't work for them. Over the months, frustration and strain grew in their marriage. Heidi put up a brave front, but most of the time she was living the harried life of a single mom, working a part-time job, and running the household by herself. Except for his monthly visits, their connections consisted of phone calls, emails, and internet video chats.

"Even though I was in a good church, I still wasn't in a good place emotionally," Brad recalled. "All that pride, defensiveness, and bitterness were still resident in me. And that led to a sense of entitlement. Adam and Eve had a feeling of entitlement in the garden — they believed God was holding out on them and that they deserved better.

"Well, I felt I deserved to feel good, to be appreciated, to feel loved, but Heidi and I weren't connecting. I should have been honest in communicating that to her because we're problem-solvers — we could have figured out what to do. But the reality is that when you take the first whiff of the apple, if you keep sniffing it, you're going to eat it."

The apple came in the form of an email from a married woman in Michigan who said she wanted help in getting back on track with her faith. Brad encouraged her to talk to a pastor at her church, but she said she related better to him. And for Brad, helping people spiritually is what motivated him the most.

They sent emails back and forth. He recommended devotional books for her and answered her spiritual questions. They began to have phone conversations and eventually met secretly.

"That's when the affair began?" I asked.

Brad's face steeled. "Don't call it an affair," he said. "That makes it sound like a little indiscretion. It minimizes the weight of the deception and sin. Call it what it was—adultery."[3]

Feeling the Weight

I felt like a therapist, sitting in a chair with a notepad, as Brad confessed the ugliest episode of his life, all while Heidi was sitting next to him. "I'm guessing you never suspected anything," I said to her.

Her voice was soft. "I had no reason not to trust him."

"Of course," Brad said. "I was the last person she would think would do what I did."

He sighed heavily, then went on. "Even on my way to the first encounter, I knew I should turn around, run the other way, get out. And I chose to press through. I felt entitled—that's how deceived I was. And to make it worse, I had the sense that God wouldn't let this destroy my ministry because it would harm the church."

He shook his head in disgust. "I can't believe I ever thought that! Did I believe that God was somehow going to protect my sin? God won't be mocked. The Bible says God didn't deal with the sin of the Amorites because their sin hadn't reached its full measure. Sometimes we think we're getting away with something, but God is waiting. Will we repent on our own? Or will our sin reach its full measure and then we come under his discipline?"

The words caught in Brad's throat. He fought back sobs. "When it started, I thought, *What have I done? What have I gotten myself into? Stop immediately, don't go any farther.* But part of me didn't want to stop, and I had the unknown of how the other person was going to react. If I left the relationship right away, how would she respond? What would she do? You can't count on the other person, because we were two self-centered people being deceptive. We were lying at our core, so we really couldn't trust each other.

"The fear of us being discovered was just horrible. *Horrible!* When I preached, I felt hypocritical, I felt empty, I felt like I was going through the motions—and I was. I had no power. The Holy Spirit wasn't anointing my ministry."

Heidi spoke up. "One weekend after I moved to South Carolina I went to church and watched Brad preach. I remember sitting there and thinking, *What's wrong with him?* He had no energy, no passion. Physically, he was hunched over. I thought—well, maybe he's tired. In retrospect, I think it was literally the weight of sin bearing down on him."

"The shame, the guilt—you're right, they were so heavy," said Brad. "Every time before I'd get up to preach, I'd confess everything to God—and then I'd confess again and again. And then afterward, I went back to the charade. A piece of me had become callous because I was shutting out the voice of God in my life."

For three months, the adultery dragged on. "About halfway through the relationship, I was looking for a good breaking point. I figured that when my family moved to South Carolina, that would be the time to stop."

But his sin reached its full measure. Brad had been found out. "It was then that I called a Christian counselor. He said to me, 'You've got to tell Heidi. And when you do, have your suitcase packed and in your car, because it's very likely she's going to tell you to leave.'"

"What were you thinking when he said that?"

Brad hesitated. "That he was right," he said. "That I've lost my marriage, I've lost my family, I've lost the church, I've lost my ministry —everything. I've lost it all."

He swallowed hard. "I remember sitting by the beach, looking out at the Atlantic Ocean," he said, "and I kept thinking how good it would be just to start swimming—and never come back to shore."

The Downward Spiral

Suicidal thoughts didn't last long. "I didn't want to be a coward," he told me. "I needed to face what I'd done."

One evening as Brad was standing on one side of the bed and Heidi on the other, he finally said, "There's something I need to talk with you about."

"What is it?" she asked.

He dropped down, almost to his knees, leaning over the bed. "I've been unfaithful to you."

The first words out of her mouth: "*What?* With whom?"

The next moments are a blur. Heidi was in shock. Almost immediately, she vomited. She wouldn't be able to eat for four days. Raw and confusing thoughts flooded into her. *I ought to kill him! I ought to kill myself. He's going to lose his job. Everything will be gone. How will we pay the bills? What about the children? Where should I go? What should I do? Can I trust him about anything? Oh, God, I need you now —more than ever.*

Heidi's eyes got big as she relived that moment. "I was furious, I was confused, I was frightened, and at the same time I was scrambling to decide what to do next, because I knew our future was over, at least as far as we had envisioned it."

Brad's bags were packed, but Heidi didn't throw him out that night. Her reason was pragmatic: she didn't want a hotel bill when she knew their income was going to plummet.

"It was obvious that he wasn't thinking clearly, and I knew that one of us had to," she told me.

Two days later, Brad met with the leaders of the South Carolina church. Brad resigned and had to endure the disgrace of informing the congregation that Sunday. All his years of preparation for the ministry and his success in the pulpit were dashed.

Brad also had to confess to his son and two daughters, who were devastated by the news. He had to tell Heidi's parents and his own parents. "It broke their hearts because they'd been so proud of me for all those years," he said.

They had to give up the house they'd been living in and for a while had nowhere to go. Finally, they moved into the upstairs of an elderly couple's home. They lost their health insurance. They lost their retirement savings. They lost ninety percent of their income. They still had to pay the mortgage on their Michigan house, which they eventually sold for a loss.

Heidi kept working at her job, which provided minimal income. As for Brad, all of his professional preparation had focused on the ministry; he lacked the skills needed for meaningful employment elsewhere, especially during tough economic times. Finally he was hired to sell airtime for a local television station, earning so little that some weeks he didn't make enough to cover his gas and phone bills. Before it was all over, he would sell his own blood plasma 110 times. He still has the scars on his arms.

"I remember seeing a candy bar in the grocery store and thinking, *I can't even afford one of those*," said Heidi. Family members volunteered to make the monthly payments on their daughter's braces.

"One of the worst moments," Heidi said, "was when I asked my counselor if we should be tested for sexually transmitted diseases, and he said, 'Absolutely.' So Brad and I went to a doctor's office. It was humiliating to ask the nurse for that test. I was so angry with Brad; I didn't even want to sit next to him. I was thinking, *I've been faithful to you, I was a virgin before you, and now I have to get tested for HIV?* It was embarrassing, it was unfair — "

Brad interjected, "It was one more awful and humiliating consequence of my sin."

Still, while they were recounting the implosion of their lives, I noticed that Heidi had quietly taken Brad's hand. As they sat beside each other, not many years downstream from the crisis that nearly capsized their relationship, I could detect no animosity or bitterness. Somehow, against so many odds, they had moved from infidelity to reconciliation, from hurt to healing.

I needed to know how.

Heidi's Story: Offering Grace after Betrayal

Despite the depth of her pain and the devastating fallout from Brad's adultery, Heidi made it clear to me that the journey toward full forgiveness began with a single step—a decision of her will, borne out of her strong and vibrant relationship with Jesus.

She had been taught that forgiveness was never optional in the Christian faith; it was required by God. This was easy to accept when trivial transgressions were involved, but now she was facing a test like never before—would she continue to walk with her Savior, or would she choose at this moment to break stride?

"My conclusion was that Christians don't get to pick and choose what they want to forgive and what they don't," she said. "The Bible says, 'Forgive as the Lord forgave you.'[4] I didn't see any wiggle room in that. As Christ had forgiven me for my sins, I needed to offer grace to Brad. Otherwise, bitterness would consume me—and bitterness is poison in the soul of a Christian. I didn't know if our marriage could be saved, but I knew I needed to forgive him."

"So forgiveness was a matter of obedience?" I asked.

"Initially, yes. I was committed to following Christ, even when it got hard. My relationship with Brad was already damaged; I didn't want my relationship with God to become strained because I refused to follow him when times were tough."

"Did you feel like forgiving Brad?"

"No, not at all. I was hurting too much. But I was determined to forgive. I knew that if I made the choice to offer forgiveness, the feelings might eventually follow. *Maybe*. But grace is a decision before it's an emotion."

"You make it sound pretty easy."

"Well, it was anything but. It was emotionally painful for me to forgive Brad, it was mentally painful, it was physically painful, it was relationally painful—but it didn't compare to the pain Jesus endured for me on the cross when he purchased my forgiveness. In light of what Christ went through, how could I withhold forgiveness from Brad?"

"In a sense," I said, "forgiveness served both of you."

"You're right. Stewing in bitterness wouldn't be good for me emotionally, spiritually, or physically. And forgiveness opened the door to the possibility—and it was just a possibility—that we might be reconciled as husband and wife."

Some partners don't want to hear the details of their spouse's cheating. They're too visual; they don't want to invite those images into their minds. But for Heidi, who is more cerebral, it was important to understand exactly how Brad had transgressed.

"I wanted to know what I was forgiving," she said. "How could I forgive him if I didn't know what happened? I didn't want something new to come out six months or six years down the road."

During their intensive therapy with a Christian counselor, and on long walks they would take together at night, Heidi pried the entire sordid story out of Brad.

Said Brad, "There were times when she would think I had told everything, but there were some details I withheld, because I was afraid if I let everything all out at once, she would walk out."

"I just didn't want any more surprises," Heidi said. "At this point, I was so hurt that I didn't care how much more painful it was. My attitude was, 'Let's just hit rock bottom and take it from there.'"

I asked Brad, "Did you feel a sense of relief in getting everything out in the open?"

"Mainly, it was embarrassing," he said. "Having your sin exposed is humiliating."

It took eighteen painful days for Brad to disclose all the details of his cheating. "In the end, I only had to ask Heidi for forgiveness once," he said. "Kind of like with Jesus—I only had to ask once."

Although Heidi spoke the words of forgiveness out of obedience, and she meant them as much as she could at the time, it took much longer to feel forgiveness toward him.

"I was still angry," she said, "but in the Christian life we can never fully rely on our feelings. Sometimes our emotions can impede us from doing what's right before the Lord. I had to ask God to help my feelings match the forgiveness that was in my heart. Yeah, the feelings took much longer. That was a process."

She also faced the issue of whether she would remain in the marriage. Brad wanted to reconcile; Heidi knew it would be her choice whether they stayed together.

"Restoration doesn't look the same for everybody," she said. "Some marriages can't be saved. Trust is gone for good. Whether we stayed together or got divorced, I had a lot of good years with Brad. He was still the father of my children, he'd be a grandfather someday—we would still have a legacy, one way or the other.

"Basically, I needed assurance that he wasn't going to do this again. Was he going to be a serial offender? Were we going to have another issue like this in two or three years? I would be better off ending the marriage at this point than in the future. I'd say it took about two months for me to decide to stay in the relationship."

"What prompted that decision?" I asked.

"Seeing Brad's remorse and repentance. He was clearly broken by all of this. That started to restore my trust. And I know God hates divorce; for me, splitting up was a last resort. I told God, 'You're going to have to help me. Mold my heart and mind. Draw me closer to you. Help me to be loving like you are.'"

"And did he answer that prayer?"

The instant I asked that question, Heidi broke down weeping. Brad slipped his arm around her shoulder; she dabbed her eyes with a handkerchief.

"Oh, yeah," she said between sobs. "The next year was the biggest growth ever in my spiritual life—I mean *huge*. I learned so many life-changing lessons—not just about marriage, but about God and his goodness and his faithfulness and his grace. That part I wouldn't trade for anything. I wouldn't be the person I am today if I hadn't gone through that. I never would have chosen it, but God used that experience to draw me closer to him than ever before.

"God gave me hope in so many ways, right when I needed it most. Like, when we were broke, I'd stop at the post office on the way home from work, and there would be a card of encouragement from a friend with some money tucked inside. Or people I knew—wonderful, godly church leaders—would confide in me that twenty years earlier they had gone through the same thing, and God had healed them and their marriages.

"In a hundred ways, God let me know he was there, that he cared, that he is the God of healing and reconciliation. I didn't have to go through this alone," she said.

She glanced at Brad, then her eyes met mine. "Honestly," she said, "I couldn't have."

Brad's Story: Receiving Grace — And Giving Grace to Himself

Broken and repentant, full of regret and remorse, Brad had no illusions about the depth of his sin and the noxious consequences that were befalling him and his family. Was he forgiven by Christ? Yes, because God's grace covers the most vile of transgressions. Was he forgiven by Heidi? Yes, because of her fidelity to Christ's teachings despite Brad's infidelity to her.

But *experiencing* forgiveness and *feeling* liberated from shame and self-condemnation — those were far more difficult for Brad to achieve.

"You can only experience God's grace to the degree that you're willing to accept full responsibility for what you've done," Brad said to me. "Could I try to find excuses? Sure. I could look back at how depleted I was, at how others weren't appreciating me, at the stress of the church, at the fact that our marriage wasn't doing well — but there have been people in far worse situations who have stayed faithful to Jesus.

"I didn't. I failed. I made the choices that I made. I can't point the finger at anyone else. Remember how Heidi had to understand the details of what I had done to fully forgive me? Well, I needed to completely accept responsibility for what I had done so I could feel fully forgiven by God. That's why I needed to stand up in front of the congregation and admit my sin without equivocation. Also, they needed to hear it from me to protect against gossip and people taking sides. I didn't want more damage done to the church."

"Has it been a struggle to stop living in shame?"

He nodded. "Absolutely. Shame says that you didn't merely sin, but that you are an irredeemable sinner — that you're forever worthless as a person, that your core identity is hopelessly soiled, that God can never use you again. I can't prevent those emotions from coming up, but I can choose to deal with them in a biblical way."

"How so?"

"I remind myself that shame is not from God. What I did in the past was sinful, but it does not define who I am now, and it doesn't define my future. Romans 8:1 says, 'Therefore, there is now no condemnation for those who are in Christ Jesus.'

"I can have grief, but that's not shame. I can have a sense of loss, but that's not shame. I can regret the consequences of what I did, but that's not shame. The fact is, I hurt a lot of people. I can't undo that. I can feel remorse over it—and I do and I will—but the moment I begin feeling shame, I know that's the enemy at work.

"Christ paid for my sins on the cross. When I'm stuck in shame, that's me taking back on myself what Jesus took on himself. I'm diminishing what Christ accomplished. Jesus doesn't want me to stay punished, because he took the punishment for what I did, and that gives me the freedom to move ahead with confidence and in grace.

"The Bible says, 'If we confess our sins, he is faithful and just and will forgive us our sins and purify us from all unrighteousness.'[5] But when I take on shame, then I'm saying that I'm not really purified, that the cross was a failure, that Jesus's sacrifice for me was lacking.

"I need to get beyond the feelings of shame and focus on the *fact* that I'm free from condemnation, the *fact* that I've been made righteous in Christ, and on the *fact* that I've been purified. I want to live on those facts, not on shameful feelings."

"All of those *are* facts," I said, "but it's also a fact that God disciplines his children. After they sinned, Adam and Eve tried to avoid that by hiding from God. Was that a temptation for you?"

"Yeah, part of me wanted to flee," he replied. "I had to consciously open myself up to God's discipline, because I knew it was for my own good. Hebrews 12 says God's discipline produces holiness, righteousness, peace, and healing in us.[6] Those were four things I desperately needed.

"If I tried to wiggle out of God's discipline by running from the consequences of my sin, then I'd be resisting what God wanted to accomplish in me. Only by facing my sin could God use it to change me for the better. The Bible warns that God's discipline isn't pleasant, but in the end the changes God produces in our character are worth it. That was true for me."

"What about hiding from people? Did you want to withdraw from others to avoid embarrassment?"

"Both of us fought that impulse. It would have been easy to isolate ourselves. Sometimes when you're in pain, you don't even have the emotional energy to engage with people. But Heidi and I stayed in our small groups, we kept going to church, and we maintained relationships with Christian friends. During that time, we saw the church at its best. People prayed with us, shared wisdom with us, kept us accountable, and encouraged us.

"I remember a Southern Baptist state official who called me. He went through the list of people in the Bible who sinned, but God restored them and kept using them in ministry."

Brad's voice began to quake. "Man, I needed to hear that. He breathed hope into me. *Just maybe,* I thought, *God is big enough to take the carnage I had created and use it for his glory.*"

God, the Healer

Brad and Heidi excused themselves to get ready for dinner, and as I sat there my mind started to wander. Glancing out the window, where pine trees shaded my backyard, I imagined a picnic—a fortieth-birthday party for a person whose face I couldn't make out. A couple of adult children laughed as they recounted family stories. Maybe there was even a grandchild in one of their arms.

It's the anniversaries that trigger my memories. Four decades earlier, a frightened friend stopped me on the University of Missouri campus. *I'm pregnant, and my boyfriend has walked away. What should I do? Lee, I trust your advice. Tell me what I should do.*

I was so flip, so cavalier in my opinions. *Well, if the baby's in your way, get rid of it. Abortion is legal in New York. I can help you make the arrangements. We'll find the money for it. It's not a big deal.*

When I came to faith in Christ a decade later, there were a lot of regrets I nailed to the cross. I knew that God's grace covered them all. Yet like Brad, forgiving myself was another matter. I was tortured by the "might have beens."

What would this child have been like? Who would he have become? As friends and family offered a toast on his fortieth birthday, what stories would they have told about the ways he had blessed them? Or maybe the child would have been a girl who grew into a woman, a mother who had ushered more lives into the world.

Over time, I kept reminding myself of the fullness of God's forgiveness, and that helped. Still, it was hard to ward off the shame. So finally I decided to write a letter to the child. I told him I was sorry. I said I wished I could go back and undo what I had done. Most of all, I said I was looking forward to being with him in heaven.

I can't remember what happened to that letter. I kept it for a long time, but then it was gone. In a way, I'm glad it's not here anymore. Christ has forgiven me. He acts as if this never happened. His grace has eased my shame. Yet my sin still echoes through time. It's the birthdays that are hardest for me.

Brad's affair—no, his adultery—will have consequences into the future. Maybe a member of his church, disillusioned by Brad's failure, has walked away from the faith. Certainly the effects of sin should never be whitewashed. Nevertheless, Brad was right about this—God is big enough to redeem even the most hurtful of sins and use the circumstances for good.

One day when Brad and Heidi were in counseling, the therapist told them, "Your marriage will emerge better because of all this."

Brad and Heidi laughed.

The counselor said, "Someday you'll use this to help other people."

They laughed again.

"If you think we'll ever talk about this publicly," said Heidi, "you're dead wrong."

He replied, "We'll see."

Can You Help Us?

On a sweltering summer day in rural Ohio, more than fifteen thousand people were attending a Christian music festival. Between acts, hundreds of them would crowd into tents to hear speakers on a variety of topics.

Three sessions were being taught by the new pastor of a nearby church and his wife. They had moved to the area after a couple of years in South Carolina. Calling their ministry "Build Your Marriage," they talked about communication, intimacy, and conflict resolution; unlike many of their events, this time the subject of adultery wasn't on the agenda.[7]

After one session, a woman — her sheepish husband in tow — came up to the speakers, Brad and Heidi. "I don't know if you can help us, but three months ago my husband revealed that he had an affair," the woman said. "And I don't know if there's any hope for us."

Heidi couldn't hold back a sympathetic smile.

"Yes," Heidi assured her, "we can help."

CHAPTER 8

The Prodigal

The Gateway to Grace Is Repentance

We can't truly appreciate God's grace until we glimpse his greatness. We won't be lifted by his love until we're humbled by his holiness.

Drew Dyck[1]

Years ago, my friend Mark Mittelberg and I were sitting on either side of Luis Palau, the affable, indefatigable evangelist, as we dined at a rustic restaurant in suburban Chicago. Somewhere between the rainbow trout and the apple crisp, as if he were suddenly gripped by an urgent impulse, Luis reached out and clasped our forearms.

"Friends, I have a favor to ask," he said in his Argentinian accent. "Would you pray for my son Andrew? He's far from the Lord, and we're very concerned about him."

I'm not sure that Luis meant for us to put down our forks and pray right then — but we did. We felt too awkward to ask for details, so we simply paused to ask God to open Andrew's heart to grace. How could we not? The expression of fatherly concern on Luis' face made it clear that even though he had told multitudes around the globe about Jesus, this was the individual he most ached to reach.

Andrew is the third of four sons born to Luis and Pat Palau. In his early years, Luis translated for Billy Graham and then went on to become one of his generation's most renowned evangelists, with his outreach festivals, books, and radio programs now having reached a billion people in seventy-five countries.[2]

When Andrew was born in 1966, his grandmother, confined to a wheelchair from polio, made a spontaneous prediction to her son-in-law Luis. Whether it was a prophetic declaration or simply wishful thinking, nobody knew, although she wasn't prone to dramatic pronouncements. Her words went down in family lore: "Luis, this one is going to be an evangelist."

Those hopes evaporated early. Though young Andrew put on a Christian front, only a thin façade masked his staunch indifference toward anything spiritual.

He seemed impervious to his father's pleadings about Jesus, choosing instead to worship at the altar of self. When he fell into drinking and smoking dope, as he pandered to his own selfish interests, as he was booted from a leading Christian university, as he flitted from girl to girl, as he wandered purposelessly through life, evading responsibility time after time, as he mastered the dark art of duplicity and deception, it would have been easy to give up on him.

Luis kept praying.

Every Decision a Bad One

"I was a fool," Andrew said to me more than two decades after that spontaneous prayer session I had with his father. "Proverbs has a lot to say about foolish people. Just go down the list—that was me."

The six-dozen references to fools in the Old Testament book of Proverbs paint a miserable and wretched picture. Fools hate wisdom, are complacent, bring grief to their parents, lack common sense, pursue schemes, revel in folly, are full of pride, practice deception, refuse to make amends, spurn discipline, scorn advice, and exalt themselves.[3] And that's just the start.

I mentally reviewed many of those qualities before saying to Andrew, "There's some pretty harsh stuff in there."

"No, seriously, I was the fool of Proverbs," Andrew insisted. "I squandered every opportunity, I took the path of least resistance, and I stumbled through life drunk or stoned or both. Just about every decision I made was wrong. Everything was about *me*—having fun, chasing women, partying with friends, getting into trouble. It was a competition to see who could do the craziest stuff and laugh about it the next day. If that's not being a fool, then I don't know what is."

We were sitting in a sparsely furnished office at Luis Palau's ministry, not far from the Portland, Oregon, airport. Even though he's in his forties and the father of teenagers, Andrew looks disarmingly youthful, his brown hair combed to the side and a little shaggy, his clothes casual and his eyes earnest.

I was taken aback by his blunt assessment of himself—which, frankly, sounded a lot like me in my early years. "What was driving you?" I asked. "Did you see hypocrisy in your home? Did your father neglect you or abuse you or wound you emotionally?"

"No, nothing like that. I can't blame anyone else. You see, I was in love with Andrew. I wanted to be cool so I'd be accepted by all the girls and the right guys in the right cliques. I was selfish, self-centered, self-indulgent—and I was rebellious, although not because I was angry at God."

"Did you think Christianity was true?"

"Well, this is embarrassing, but I thought it probably *was* true. The thing is, I just didn't care. I loved my sin too much."

"You must have done a good job of hiding it from your parents," I said.

"Yeah, I was very duplicitous. I would act like I was friendly and gregarious and positive. I would say all the right things—and when I had to, I'd lie to get myself out of trouble. In fact, I did everything a good evangelist's boy was supposed to do—I was part of the church's youth group, I memorized Bible verses, I went to missions conferences, and I attended church every Sunday."

"What did you think of church?"

"I kind of liked it."

"Really?"

"Sure," he replied. "People were very friendly. Besides, many of my party friends attended church. I didn't want to be accused of being a hypocrite or cause any hassle for my parents, so I just tried to move along in the Christian world. Sounds very contradictory, but I was pretty sincere in not wanting to trouble my family and others. I played it pretty well."

"Jungle Juice" and Pot

Early in life, Andrew began flirting with trouble to gain attention from the crowd he wanted to impress. First, there was petty vandalism and other reckless behavior, like blowing up jugs of gasoline on highways at night to startle drivers, igniting Molotov cocktails in the schoolyard, and building bigger and more powerful pipe bombs. Then came theft and drinking, with Andrew and his friends stealing beer from the garages and alcohol from the liquor cabinets of their neighbors. They would make "jungle juice" for their parties, a potent alcoholic concoction brewed in thirty-gallon garbage cans.

Pretty soon came marijuana. "There was a period of time in high school when we'd smoke dope on the way to school, at lunch, and then after school," Andrew said. "We would party every chance we could get, usually at a house when parents were out of town."

"Did you ever get caught?"

"Occasionally. Once in high school we were drinking, and I crashed the car in someone's front yard, and we all fled. I got a ticket for hit-and-run driving, which was a felony, though later that got resolved. Usually, I would weasel my way out of trouble. I really hated it when I was caught, and I did show remorse, but getting away with things made me even bolder the next time."

After high school, he went to conservative Biola University in

Southern California. "I relied so much on what others thought of me, and suddenly there I was at a new place where nobody knew me. I began asking, 'Who am I, really?' But instead of digging deep, I reverted to what I knew: partying and drinking."

He lasted a year until Biola "invited" him to "seek success elsewhere." He transferred to the University of Oregon in Eugene, a more liberal school, where he majored in English literature and dabbled in cocaine and hallucinogenic drugs.

"By then I was really out of control," he said. "Nobody was looking over my shoulder, so I pushed the limits. I was manipulative and deceitful to the women I was dating. On weekends, my friends and I would go to isolated sand dunes at the beach, build a fire, play music, drink beer, trip on acid, and spend the night. Eventually our fraternity was banned from campus after we torched an old Volkswagen Beetle that belonged to one of our frat brothers."

His classes weren't going much better. "I liked to project the image of being an intellectual, but actually I was shallow and knew just enough about literature to fool someone who didn't know any better," he said. "I was still unsure of my personal identity. I'd worn so many masks for so long that when I looked in the mirror, I didn't recognize who was looking back."

Seeking to break the downward spiral, Luis suggested that Andrew drop out of school and go to Europe to gain some life experience. Andrew worked at an upscale clothing store in Cardiff, Wales (taking time off to bum around the Continent, smoke hashish, and stow away on a ship), and then moved to Northern Ireland, where he worked at a furniture store.

A Letter from a Father

"My life was headed nowhere," Andrew said, "but my dad never stopped pursuing me. When I was young, he would take me for walks and tell me about Jesus. Wherever I moved, he would have his friends take me to dinner and share Christ with me. And he would write me letters."

Andrew slipped on some glasses and picked up a copy of his book *The Secret Life of a Fool,* in which he tells his story.[4] "I especially remember a letter he wrote before he visited me in Northern Ireland," he said. "It really shows his heart."

He flipped to the right page and read excerpts aloud to me, his voice laden with emotion:

> Dear Andrew ...
>
> There's a phrase that keeps coming back to me every time I pray for you and think about you (and I do that very much as you can imagine—you are a son I love very much). When I was 21 like you I took this little phrase for myself: "But you, man of God ..." 1 Timothy 6:11.
>
> You were born, Andrew, to be a man of God. That's what God has for you. That is God's purpose for your life.... The Lord God loves you with an everlasting love. The first step he has taken to bring you to himself is that he went willingly and personally for you to a cross. On that cross he became your substitute. He took your place and your punishment and forever removed your guilt.
>
> I pray first of all, Andrew, that you would open your heart to Jesus Christ for sure. The day I prayed and asked Christ to give me eternal life a counselor used Romans 10:9–10 with me. He personalized it just for me. I've never asked you, Andrew: have you ever asked him personally?
>
> If you confess with your lips, Andrew, that Jesus is Lord and believe in your heart, Andrew, that God raised Jesus from the dead, you, Andrew, shall be saved. For it is with your heart, Andrew, that you believe and are justified and it is with your

mouth that you confess, Andrew, and are saved. Then verse 13—
"For everyone who calls on the name of the Lord will be saved."

If you haven't made that decision for sure, Andrew, and if you
want me to help pray with you—and nothing would give me
greater joy in the whole world—I would do it ... if you want.

Secondly, a little phrase came to me a short while ago: the
secret life is the secret. What you are in your soul is what you
really are. As a man thinks in his heart, so he is, says the book
of Proverbs.[5] You will become a man of God, Andrew, when
you specifically and clearly invite Christ into your soul. You
develop your inner secret life with your heavenly Father on your
knees, reading God's word; on your knees, talking to God in
prayer; on your knees, singing and praising God, committed to
obedience. ...

Andrew, my love for you as my son is very deep. The potential
I see in your life as God has made you is superb. You could bless
and change and bring great happiness and eternal life to millions
if you obey Jesus Christ as your Master and Lord.

"Follow me and I will make you fishers of men."[6] I took that
quote from Jesus very seriously at your age. I love it. It's the best
life in the world. You will enjoy it, too, my son, if you follow
Jesus with all your heart and soul. What else is there in this
rebellious world? Not much.

> See you soon. I love you and pray for you,
> Dad[7]

Andrew let the word "Dad" linger for a few moments, then closed
the book, set it on the desk, and slipped his glasses into a shirt pocket.

"That's my father," he said finally. "The same things he said to a
hundred thousand people, he said to his son. He knew that the only
thing that could change my life would be God's grace. He saw that so
clearly, but I was so blind to it. His confidence has always been in the
power of the Gospel."

The Panhandler and the Nightclub

Fast forward a few years. By now Andrew was living in Boston, start-ing on the bottom rung of the corporate ladder at a clothing retailer, and living on a tight budget in a cramped apartment. He remained as far from God as ever.

"I found myself relying on alcohol and partying for different rea-sons," he said. "I was using them to mask the reality of all the guilt and shame in my life. I didn't like to go to bed sober, because then I'd be haunted by memories of all the people I had hurt or deceived or used. And there was anxiety—fear of the future, fear of the world, fear of eternity."

"How bad did things get?"

"Emotionally, I was despondent," he replied. "Fewer and fewer people were impressed by my antics. I was always partying, which was a little embarrassing for someone my age. If I couldn't find anyone to go out drinking with me, I'd get drunk on beer and watch television until I fell asleep on the couch. When I'd wake up, the fuzz would be on the screen—those were the days when stations would sign off in the early morning hours. I'd turn off the TV, go to bed, the alarm would go off, I'd go to work and then repeat the cycle."

"Did you ever think about spiritual matters?"

Andrew's eyes narrowed as he thought back. "I was starting to wonder about eternity—like, would my life someday just turn to fuzz like the TV and that would be it? It was a demoralizing thought."

"When did you hit bottom?"

"Two things happened. Some friends and I were out drinking and carousing one night, and we got into a profane shouting match with a panhandler on a sidewalk. After a while he laid down to sleep, and I can't believe we did this, but we started kicking him, repeatedly."

He grimaced. "I mean, how low can a person get—kicking a

homeless person?" he said. "Really, I'm ashamed to even tell the story. How did I descend to where I thought that was okay? That was probably my lowest point. And then something bizarre happened in a nightclub that really shook me."

"A nightclub?"

"Yeah, a huge, warehouse-type place—a techno-pop dance club. It was pretty dark and people were everywhere. I was headed to the bathroom when a guy sort of grabbed me and said, 'You're a believer.' I said, 'What are you talking about?' He repeated, 'You're a believer, right?'"

"Was it someone you knew?" I asked.

"No, that was the odd part. I was thinking maybe he recognized me from church when I was a kid, or maybe he was a friend of my dad's. I thought, *Oh no, this is awful. This guy thinks I'm a Christian, and he wants to talk about it.* I was desperate to get away from him. So I said, 'Yeah, I'm a believer,' hoping to satisfy him and get out of a conversation."

"How did he respond?"

"He said, 'I knew it. You're a follower of Satan, right?' And he smiled—sort of an enigmatic grin—and walked away into the crowd. I started protesting, saying, 'No, no, no,' but he was gone. It was chilling to me."

I pondered the bizarre scene. "What did you make of it?"

"I was haunted by it. What did he see in me that made him think I was a follower of Satan? Or could this have been some sort of supernatural encounter? It seemed demonic, like I was engaging something very dark. I felt like, on the one hand, there was my dad pursuing me for God, and now on the other hand there seemed to be this other reality that was clawing after me."

I was struck by the imagery. "What kind of impact did this have on you?" I asked. "Did it cause you to turn to God?"

"It probably should have. It certainly left a big impression. For a long time I wondered whether my lifestyle of drugs and booze had opened a gateway into another world. And certainly that's possible."

He shook his head, dismayed with himself. "But like so many other times in my life, after a while I simply moved on—down the same twisted road I had been traveling all along."

A Decision, but Hesitation

Luis Palau can be clever. He waited until the winter temperature in Boston was unbearably cold, and then he called to invite Andrew to one of his evangelistic rallies. When Andrew demurred as usual, insisting he wasn't interested, Luis casually let it be known that the event would be in Jamaica. Once Luis agreed to set up a marlin-fishing trip for him, Andrew was starting to pack his bags.

Andrew's mind danced with images of guzzling beer in the Caribbean sunshine, but Luis had another motive: he wanted one more shot at breaking through his son's seemingly intractable spiritual resistance.

Andrew ended up staying with a Jamaican businessman and his family, which included son Chris and daughter Wendy. As Andrew hung around with them and their friends, he was amazed—and intrigued—by their fresh and enthusiastic faith, which seemed to reflect the "abundant life" he had always heard his parents talk about.[8]

"They were fun and normal, warm and friendly, engaged with the community, and they were sold out to Christ in a very winsome and radical way," Andrew recalled. "Jesus seemed so real and present to them. I was listening as they told others about how God had healed their addictions and restored their relationships—and I was thinking, *This is what I need! I can't keep pretending that my shame and guilt aren't dogging me. Something has got to happen.*"

On three of the five nights when Luis was preaching at the Kingston National Stadium, a 35,000-seat sports facility next to the famous statue of reggae singer Bob Marley, Andrew attended with his new friends.

"I always respected dad and the sincerity of his message," Andrew told me. "On the last night of the crusade, I went with a receptive attitude. I really wanted to hear the voice of the God who had so completely changed the lives of these new friends of mine."

"And did you?"

"Well, as I sat there and listened, it struck me that Dad's message was different than ever before. It was like he was picking on me. He really went after me. And then I realized: this was the same message he almost always gives. He was talking about the story of the rich young ruler—only, I wasn't rich and I ruled nothing.[9] It had nothing to do with me, and yet the Lord was pressing me.

"When he gave the invitation to receive Christ, I found myself saying in my spirit, *Lord, This is what I want. Please come into my life. I'm going a new direction. I want heaven, and I want to do the right thing. Everything I say I hate but I can't stop doing—I want to stop doing it. Everything I say I want to do but can't seem to do—I want to do it.* At that moment, I determined to stop drinking, break off my inappropriate relationships, and start going to church."

"Were you sincere?"

"Yes, it was genuine. I wanted what God was offering. I realized it was so much better than the empty life I had been leading."

Luis typically caps his rallies with a call for people to come forward if they want to follow Christ. "Did you respond to the altar call?" I asked.

"I felt compelled to go, but I resisted. A lot of people did walk forward, though, and many of them were sobbing. I thought, *Something must really be wrong with them.* I figured my decision was more cerebral than theirs. But to me, I was taking a bold step. Afterward I felt a sense of relief. I immediately told Wendy, and she was thrilled. She said I needed to tell my parents."

"How did you feel about doing that?"

"I felt some trepidation, honestly. As my dad remembers it, I bounded into their hotel room and declared, 'I did it! I did it! I've become a Christian!' As I recall, though, the conversation felt awkward."

"In what way?"

"I told them about my decision and of course they were very encouraging and affirming. They'd seen this kind of response in people at a lot of their crusades over the years, and they knew that what God started, he would somehow complete.[10] But there was also some hesitation on their part—a little bit of a wait-and-see attitude."

"Hmmm. Was it warranted?"

"Well," he replied, "based on what happened next, it was pretty discerning on their part."

The Effects of "Cheap Grace"

Andrew's friends in Boston were astonished—and skeptical—when he told them he was now a Christian. They watched warily as he went to church and started to clean up his life. But the "new Andrew" lasted only a month.

"One night I went out with some friends to a bar—not to drink, but just to hang out," Andrew said to me. "Pretty soon I had a beer. Then another. Then six, plus three straight shots. And I started smoking dope. Before long, I was involved again with some of the girls I knew I should be avoiding."

"So everything fell apart?"

"Completely. I embarrassed myself—and the Lord. My friends were laughing at me. I was ashamed and humiliated. My life started to spiral downward again. I kept thinking, *How could my commitment*

to God have been so real to me—and now this? How could I have been so
sincere and yet fail so badly? And what was I supposed to do now?"

"Looking back, how do you analyze what happened?"

"It turns out I had more in common with the rich young ruler than
I thought. Jesus challenged him to give himself wholly to God, but
he wouldn't give up his wealth. He insisted on clinging to it, even if it
meant walking away from Jesus. Well, I had built my own kingdom
of pleasure, where I reigned supreme. I didn't really want God to rule
all of my life; I wanted to hang onto the partying and the so-called
fun stuff."

"Still," I said, "the prayer in Jamaica was a step in the right
direction."

"Yeah, it was a step. My heart seemed to be opening to God. But
as I look back at it, my prayer in Jamaica was hollow. A salvation
prayer doesn't mean much unless you authentically turn from sin and
allow God to take over your life. *That's* what he deserves. Contrary to
what my dad was preaching, I was only winking at God. I was saying,
I want all the good things you offer—the forgiveness, the release from
guilt, heaven, and all that—and I'll try my hardest to do good to keep
you happy and get the things I genuinely desire. Yes, I want you, God, but
without giving up me. Is it a deal?"

Shaking his head, he said: "God doesn't bargain like that. Not at
all. This was the cheap grace that Bonhoeffer warned about."

I recognized the reference. Cheap grace, said German theologian
Dietrich Bonhoeffer, "is the grace we bestow on ourselves. Cheap
grace is ... forgiveness without requiring repentance ... [and] absolu-
tion without personal confession. Cheap grace is grace without discipleship, grace without the cross, grace without Jesus Christ living and
incarnate."[11] We must seek "costly grace," urged Bonhoeffer, because
"what has cost God much cannot be cheap to us." It is costly because
it condemns sin, he wrote, but it is grace because it saves the sinner.[12]

"Lord, I'm Open"

Wendy was the reason Andrew went back to visit Jamaica many months later. He had been captivated by her charm and intrigued by her deep and abiding faith in Christ. When Andrew got together with her and her friends again in the islands, he tried his best to act like a Christian. It didn't take them long to see through his charade.

One of them, Steve, confronted Andrew one evening: "May I ask you something? What's *really* going on with you?"

Andrew was busted—he knew they had discerned that he wasn't following Jesus. So he admitted that he was struggling spiritually and had botched his efforts to lead a better life.

"I was surprised that Steve didn't panic or get on my case," Andrew told me. "He said it wasn't unusual to need to grow after an initial decision for Christ, and he invited me to pray and read the Bible with him the next morning."

On their knees at dawn, Steve read the opening verses of Romans 12: "Therefore, I urge you, brothers and sisters, in view of God's mercy, to offer your bodies as a living sacrifice, holy and pleasing to God—this is your true and proper worship. Do not be conformed to the pattern of this world, but be transformed by the renewing of your mind. Then you will be able to test and approve what God's will is —his good, pleasing and perfect will."[13]

As they began to discuss the passage, Andrew started to weep out of frustration. He had heard the words, but their meaning eluded him.

"My comprehension level was zero," he said to me. "There I was —an English literature major who was used to interpreting texts, but I had absolutely no idea what this passage meant. I really wanted to hear from God through his Word, but it was like there was a wall between me and the verses."

Steve continued to try to explain what the apostle Paul was teaching in the passage. At the time, Andrew was thinking to himself, *I tried this Christianity thing, and I failed. I'm not sure what these verses mean when they talk about transformation and renewal—but whatever it is, it certainly isn't happening to me.*

Seeing Andrew's exasperation, Steve offered a solution: "You need to come up to the mountain."

He said that every year a group of Christians went on a retreat to the lush and tropical Blue Mountains outside Kingston for a few days of building friendships, prayer, worship, and teaching from the Bible.

It would require some last-minute changes to his itinerary, but Andrew felt drawn to the experience. Silently, he prayed: *Lord, I'm open. Let's face it: I've opened myself up to all the garbage of the world —why wouldn't I open myself up to whatever you have for me?*

Andrew said to Steve: "I'll do it."

Confession and Cleansing

At the two-day gathering, the teaching focused on grand and lofty themes—the greatness and power of God, the authority of God, his holiness and divine character, and the biblical picture of God as Creator and King of the universe. There was discussion about the Holy Spirit's work in the world, convicting people of sin, drawing them to God's kingdom, and transforming them from the inside.

More and more, Andrew wanted to experience, personally and intimately, this awesome God as others at the retreat had done. *What's it going to take?* he kept asking God. *If you're real—if all this is true —then I have to know for sure.*

He began begging God for a supernatural encounter. *Lord, just do this one more thing: Reveal yourself to me. Stand before me and I'll know you're real. You can do that, for sure. You've got the power. Then I'll believe and I'll never forget.*

Over and over, he implored God to appear. He thought that if he could somehow muster maximum sincerity, if he wanted it with his whole heart, and God didn't respond—then maybe it was time to give up once and for all.

Just appear before me, Lord. Just do this one more thing, he prayed fervently—forgetting that Jesus, on the cross, declared, "It is finished," and now waits for people to respond in faith.

Despite Andrew's pleas—nothing.

Frustrated and discouraged, almost as a last-ditch effort, as if he were throwing up his arms in exasperation, Andrew abruptly found himself changing his prayer. *God,* he whispered, *what is keeping me from you?*

Instantly, he was startled by a distinct response he felt in his spirit. *Do you really want to know, Andrew?* Now he was ever more eager; here was the divine engagement he had been so earnestly seeking; finally, perhaps God would appear to him. *Yes, God, of course. What is it? What's keeping me from you?*

Andrew's eyebrows raised as he described to me what happened next, as if he were freshly reliving the moment; his words came tumbling out, his tone a mix of astonishment and wonder—and horror.

"Immediately, in a flash—and this is hard to put into words—God miraculously opened my eyes to what had been keeping us apart: there before me was all the garbage of my life, all of my lying, cheating, stealing, and abusive relationships, all the arrogance and pride, all the addictions and people I had hurt, all the deception and hypocrisy and callousness—I saw it all, this seemingly insurmountable pile of sin stacked as high as I could see.

"I was stricken, I was horrified—I gasped and fell on my face, embarrassed and humiliated and remorseful, bawling like I never had before. I was heaving with sobs; my tears were falling on the floor. *God,* I said, *how could I have been such a fool? Please forgive me! Please take this away! I can't live with it anymore. What hope do I have when all of this garbage is in me?*

"And God's response in that moment was right out of Scripture: *If*

*you confess your sin, Andrew, I am able to forgive you of your unrighteous-
ness. I will clean it out. I will take it as far as the east is from the west. I
will remember your sin no more.*

"I started confessing as fast as God could bring my sins into my
consciousness; he would unveil them to me, one after the other, and
I would cry out for forgiveness, and he would release them. He was
cleaning me, scrubbing me, scouring me. I saw myself as I really was,
in light of his holiness and purity, and like Isaiah before the throne
of the Lord, I was shattered.[14] But by his grace, God was piecing me
back together.

"So there I was, face down on the floor, and some of the guys came
over and put their arms on my shoulder and said, 'This is your time,
Andrew. Make sure you get it all out. Don't try to hide anything from
the Lord.' They brought me to a room and helped me verbalize some
of my confession.

"After two or three hours, it was over—and it was like God had
flipped on a light in my soul. I felt such incredible relief—an utter
sense of release from all the things that had entrapped me. For the
first time, I understood what Jesus meant when he said he will not
only make us free, but *free indeed*—like a captive not only released
from prison but running into the arms of his father. I looked out at
the mountain, and it was as if the whole world was fresh and new
—beautiful, just beautiful.

"I kept thanking God for his grace, and then, out of sheer gratitude, I whispered, 'I will tell everyone what you have done.' As the
words left me, he replied, *You will*—not in the form of a question, but
more of a statement, like he was sealing his calling on my life.

"So I was celebrating and thanking God, and I remember having
this strong impression in my spirit that God was saying to me, *I'm
with you, Andrew; I'm the source of your rejoicing—but don't you realize
the power of prayer that was in your life?*

"And I was like, *Yeah, of course, that's true.* I thought of all the times my parents lifted me up to the Lord through the years—and even strangers all over the world who my dad would press into praying for me."

He grinned, then pointed toward me. "Even you, Lee."

The Rebel's Only Way

This time things went differently when he told his father. "I came down the mountain and called my dad immediately," Andrew told me. "I said, 'You'll never guess what happened.' I described what God had done and he said, 'Oh, wow, Andrew—*that's* what we've been waiting for.'"

"Repentance," I said.

"Exactly—repentance is the rebel's only path to God. I needed to confess that I'm wrong and God is right; I needed to see my depravity in contrast with his holiness; I needed his cleansing and leadership of my life. *This* is how transformation and renewal begin. It's not enough just to pray, *God, make me a better person*. It was repentance that opened the floodgates of grace for me—and it was grace that changed my life and eternity."

Years after his soul-healing experience with God and subsequent studies at a seminary, now on a new path of following Jesus wholeheartedly, Andrew joined the Palau organization. He carried his father's bags for four years and then spent six years living in various cities to serve local churches and develop enormous music and sports festivals where Luis would share the gospel.

In the years since then, he has become an evangelist himself, telling the story of God's grace at rallies and festivals all around the world, sometimes speaking to crowds of tens of thousands and other times encouraging individual inmates in prison.[15]

Oh, and remember Wendy? She and Andrew have now been married for more than twenty years.

Andrew's story evoked strong memories in me. Attracted by the positive ways my wife Leslie's life changed after she became a Christian, I spent nearly two years using my legal training and journalism experience to investigate the validity of Christianity. At the time, I wasn't aware that even my ability to seek God was because his grace was already enabling me to search.[16]

If God were a mirage or a product of wishful thinking, if Jesus were a legend, a fraud, or simply a crutch for the weak—then I wanted nothing to do with Christianity. But as the evidence began to pile up, as Jesus was able to take my skeptical punches and keep bouncing back, I became more and more intrigued. And like Andrew Palau, I finally got to the point where I was wide open spiritually. After all, if God is real, why would I not want to experience him?

On the afternoon of Sunday, November 8, 1981, alone in my bedroom, I finished tallying the evidence and arguments for and against Christianity. At that moment, I reached my personal verdict in the case for Christ. But this involved more than mere intellectual assent to a set of propositions, because at the instant I realized that God is alive and that he is holy and perfect and pure, I became mortified by the corruption in my own soul.

Like Andrew, my life had been consumed by pride and self-worship, by alcohol and illicit relationships, by the arrogant disregard of others. The father of my best friend in high school once remarked that I was the most amoral person he had ever met. Nothing guided my life but my own cynical self-interest.

At that moment when my eyes were opened to God, all of my sin flooded into my mind like the discharge of a sewer. I was aghast and repulsed. I wanted to run and hide from the bright light of God's conviction. Only one thing stopped me—a verse a friend had pointed out to me earlier and which I almost instinctively sought out in that moment: "Yet to all who did receive him, to those who believed in his name, he gave the right to become children of God."[17]

Oh, God, I'm overwhelmed by my sins. Only your grace can save me. Please cleanse me, change me, lead me, use me.

In ways beyond what I ever anticipated, God answered me. Like an orphan named Stephanie and an addict named Jud, like a sinner named Craig and a killer called Duch, like a felon named Cody and a cheater named Brad, I was not only forgiven — but I was welcomed into the caring family of a Father who would never disappoint.

For the next thirty years, my life took a new path of adventure and fulfillment as God opened doors to serve him and others in ways I never could have foreseen — until one day, without warning, both my physical and spiritual health came to a crisis point.

CHAPTER 9

Empty Hands

When All Seems Lost, God's Grace Is Enough

When all seems lost, God's grace is enough.
God does not give a Gift inferior to Himself.
Augustine[1]

L eslie found me on our bedroom floor, comatose. Frantically, she
called the paramedics. I remember waking in a hospital emer-
gency room, a physician looking down at me.

"You're one step away from a coma," he said, "and two steps away
from dying."

I slipped back into unconsciousness.

An unlikely cascade of medical issues had put me on the edge of
death as I approached my sixtieth year. A routine heart procedure a
few weeks earlier had caused complications that were shutting down
my kidneys. Pneumonia was developing in my lungs. I had a rare and
severe allergic reaction to medication given to me for a voice problem.
But my doctors were unaware that any of this was going on.

What threatened my life the most was *hyponatremia*—my blood
sodium level had plummeted to the point where life was unsustain-
able. Water was entering my cells and triggering dangerous swelling of
my brain. Doctors needed to raise the level back to normal to stabilize
me, but it had to be done slowly and carefully. If it were elevated too
quickly, the brain could be irreparably damaged, leading to death or
severe disability.

Blood sodium level? I had never heard of it. Neither had anyone else in my family. As it drops further and further, symptoms become increasingly severe. Nausea, headache, fatigue, and muscle weakness are followed by disorientation and altered mental states, including hallucinations. Finally, there are seizures, unconsciousness, coma—and death.

My brain was already reacting. In the days before I fell comatose at the house, my thinking became more and more muddled and irrational. Leslie was puzzled by my behavior, which was starting to become erratic, but I managed—at first—to keep most of my bizarre thoughts to myself.

Classic symptoms of paranoia began to set in. I started to think people were eavesdropping on my conversations and plotting my downfall. *That jogger going by the house—certainly he's working undercover for the FBI.* Sounds funny to me now, but back then it seemed to make total sense. This went on for several days, with the fear and confusion getting increasingly worse.

One afternoon when Leslie went out, I sat down on the couch in our family room. It was midafternoon, not long after I had taken some medication that was inadvertently worsening my condition. I felt sapped of all energy, unable to even lift an arm. The room began to darken. An ominous and malevolent presence filled the house. My heart raced.

I was descending into hell.

Visions of Terror and Loss

The room was cold and damp. I felt suffocated by dread and hopelessness and despair. Menacing creatures began to gather at the periphery of the room and slowly inch toward me, taking their time to heighten the fear. Snakes and demons slithered on the floor; I wanted to lift my feet to escape them, but I couldn't move. It was as if my will had drained away.

I began to glimpse images of people I knew—friends and even family—their severed heads floating toward me, one after the other. As they got closer, their faces would dissolve as if drenched in acid, their mouths agape in horror.

On the wall, the clock stopped; then the minute hand began to inch backward. Deep inside, I felt what it was like to face eternity in this den of evil and terror. There was no hope of rescue, no way to escape, no relief from the panic—just an endless series of horrific tomorrows. A single minute seemed like hours.

I have no idea how long this experience lasted, but suddenly I heard the back door close. Leslie walked into the kitchen. The disturbing images disappeared. I still sat on the couch, shaken and processing what just happened. Too embarrassed to talk about it, I sat quietly as Leslie made herself a cup of tea and sat down next to me.

She took a sip and then looked at me. I was pale and breathing heavily. "Are you okay?" she asked.

My heart was breaking. "Leslie," I whispered, "do you think there will be many people in hell?"

"I don't know," she said. "Why do you bring that up?" She reached over to feel my forehead. "You're sweating. You don't look well. Why don't you lie down for a while?"

Alone in the bedroom, my yet-to-be diagnosed hyponatremia continued to worsen. I became utterly convinced that everything in my life was gone. My wife was leaving me. My children were denouncing me. My friends were abandoning me. My bank accounts were dry. The house and cars were being repossessed. Police were hunting for me for unspecified crimes. Though innocent, I was headed to prison and disgrace. I imagined myself living in a dirt field, alone, shivering against the Colorado cold, with nowhere to go and nobody to help me.

From my perspective, this was no medically induced fantasy; this was indistinguishable from reality. I felt the full emotional impact of every part of it. I have never been homeless, but in my mind I experienced what it's like to be. I have never been broke, abandoned, or ostracized, but now I knew what those feel like. I have never been imprisoned, but now I could understand the dehumanizing effects of incarceration.

I wish I could say that my instinctive reaction when my mind became unhinged was to seek Jesus, but it wasn't. As my brain was squeezed against the inside of my skull, my irrationality increased. I was overwrought with emotional turmoil over my perceived situation.

In my complete confusion, I began to think that Jesus had abandoned me like everyone else. Why wouldn't he? I was homeless, without family or friends, without anything to my name. My reputation would be destroyed, my accomplishments dashed.

I had nothing whatsoever to commend myself to God.

Reconnecting with God

The entire ordeal lasted several days before my complete collapse and hospitalization. In the midst of it all, my son Kyle came to me with a simple suggestion: "Dad, we need to pray."

Kyle was a toddler when I came to faith in Jesus, and so he didn't know me in my hard-drinking days as a spiritual skeptic. He grew up when I was a new Christian, still unlearning the unhealthy habits of my past as I opened my life more and more to the ways of Jesus. I made plenty of mistakes as a father, no doubt.

Still, Kyle found his own faith in Christ as a young man and then had a radical call to ministry during a tumultuous mission trip to the Dominican Republic, where he found himself in frightening circumstances amidst an outbreak of civil unrest.

Kyle has taken an academic route, earning an undergraduate degree in Biblical Studies, master's degrees in New Testament and Philosophy of Religion, and then a doctorate in Theology at the University of Aberdeen in Scotland. His focus has been on spiritual formation

—the way in which we become conformed to the image of Christ. It was his expertise in that area—and his concern for the confusion he could see growing in his dad—that prompted his visit to our house.

Honestly, I didn't want to pray with him. I was feeling as if God had walked away from me, like everyone else in my imagination. I had nothing to offer him. I had felt the emotional punch of what it means to be separated from God in hell—and maybe that's where I needed to end up.

Kyle and I sat in adjacent chairs. "Dad, I don't know everything that's going on with you, but I sense you're feeling alienated from God right now," he said.

"That's true."

"Well, I want to help you reconnect with your identity in Christ."

"What do you mean?"

"You see, when we approach God, we unintentionally bring along a false self, because our identity is tied up in what we do and what we accomplish. We subconsciously hide who we really are in order to project an image to God—and to the world—that we're really in control. I want to help you strip that away."

I nodded. "I want that too."

A Prayer of Honesty and Faith

For the next thirty minutes, Kyle guided me in a prayer, prompting me in specific areas and giving me time to assimilate the words and then express them myself to God. He was following the contours and even some of the language of the "Prayer of Recollection," written in various forms by his former professor, John H. Coe.[2]

Our time was filled with long pauses, as I pondered and acknowledged the truth of each statement, letting it soak into my soul before repeating it aloud to God.

"Lord, I affirm I am idolatrous and sinful and that this has leaked into how I present myself to you," Kyle began. "I admit to you that I am finite. I like to believe I'm infinite and can control life and run my world, but the truth is I can't. Only you can.

"I affirm that I am a finite physical body, and that right now I'm feeling confused and tired and a little scared. My illness has clouded my mind. My body is limited—I can't meet everyone's wishes, let alone my own ambitions and desires. I'm thankful I'm not God. Only you can meet all of my needs.

"I affirm that I'm not defined by my abilities, my roles, or my accomplishments. At my deepest places, I'm not my behaviors, my feelings, my choices, my personality quirks, my virtues, or my vices. I am not defined by how much I succeed or what other people think of me.

"At the core of my spirit, I'm not a pastor.... I'm not an author.... I'm not a speaker.... I'm not a teacher or an apologist.... I'm not my awards or honors.... I'm not my degrees.... I'm not my résumé.... I'm not a Christian celebrity.... I'm not my bank account.... I'm not my possessions or my relationships. I'm not a husband or a parent or a son or a neighbor or a friend."

As I prayed those words, I felt layers of myself peeling away—and I was relieved. I could stop pretending. I could stop trying to hold my world together by myself. I could stop acting like I had all the answers. I could come into God's presence as I really was.

"Lord," Kyle said, with me continuing to echo his words, "I affirm the reality of my soul's true identity: I am yours, God, created for union with you. In my deepest place, I am a naked spirit clothed in the righteousness of Christ. I am precious in your eyes. I am fully pardoned of my guilt and fully accepted by you. I am your son, beloved by you for eternity and held in your everlasting embrace. *That* is who I truly am."

My eyes moistened as this truth crystalized: even if I were to actually lose everything—my house, my finances, my friends, my reputation, my position—it really wouldn't matter in the end, because I would still have God's grace. I would still be the Father's adopted and beloved son. And that would be enough.

Our prayer continued for quite a while along these lines. At the end of our time together, Kyle picked up his Bible and closed with the apostle Paul's words in Philippians 3:8–9: "'I consider everything a loss because of the surpassing worth of knowing Christ Jesus my Lord, for whose sake I have lost all things. I consider them garbage, that I may gain Christ and be found in him, not having a righteousness of my own that comes from the law, but that which is through faith in Christ....'"

I thought of the angel in my childhood dream. "Someday," he said, "you'll understand." Back then, I didn't realize that my understanding would come in stages over time, as the depth and truth of God's grace would unfold in my life.

Even through the most painful of episodes.

Free Indeed

Nothing liberates like grace. I felt lighthearted after my prayer session with Kyle. I recalled the day Leslie and I got married. Neither of us were Christians at the time, but as we walked into the reception a Scottish bagpiper was playing what I later found out was "Amazing Grace."

"Catchy tune," I said.

I was oblivious to its lyrics. I never would have guessed that someday John Newton's hymn would become the theme of my life. *Amazing grace, how sweet the sound that saved a wretch like me.*

After my hyponatremia landed me in the hospital, it took several days for doctors to carefully raise my sodium level back to normal. I went through a battery of brain scans and other tests. They treated my pneumonia. My mind slowly regained clarity, although the episode did leave some lasting damage: one of my kidneys could not be saved.

One day my doctor came bounding into my room. "Everything's normal," he said. "Your levels are fine. You're free to go."

I smiled and glanced out the window at the snowcapped Rocky Mountains in the distance. *I'm free, all right*, I thought to myself. *More than he knows.*

The doctors assured me that this entire ordeal was a fluke, an extraordinary confluence of medical complications that would never recur. The hallucinations? They're typical for severe hyponatremia cases, I was told. They wouldn't come back—and yet I knew they had left their mark. God would use that bizarre experience for my ultimate good, as Romans 8:28 promises.

I would never see the homeless the same way again. Or the imprisoned. Or the ostracized and abandoned. Or those whose lives are taking them on a dangerous road away from God, toward an eternity of regret and remorse.

And I would never see myself the same again. I was determined to cling to my true identity—a son of the Most High, amazed by his grace.

EPILOGUE

Grace Withheld, Grace Extended

See to it that no one misses the grace of God.
Hebrews 12:15 NIV 1984

I always wondered: Would I cry when my father died?

After the confrontation in which my dad declared he didn't have enough love for me to fill his little finger, I stormed out of the house, determined never to return. I lived for two months in a small apartment nearly forty miles away as I worked as a reporter for a small daily newspaper. The publisher agreed to hire me beyond the summer. My future seemed set.

I never heard from my father, but my mother kept urging me to return. She would call and write to tell me my dad certainly couldn't have meant what he said. Finally, I did come home briefly, but my father and I never discussed the incident that prompted me to leave. I never broached it, and neither did he.

We maintained a civil but distant relationship through the years. He paid for my college tuition, for which I never thanked him. He never wrote, visited, or came to my graduation. When I got married after my sophomore year at the University of Missouri, my parents hosted the reception, but my dad and I never had a heart-to-heart talk.

Fresh from Missouri's journalism school, I was hired as a general assignment reporter at the *Chicago Tribune*, later developing an interest in law. I took a leave of absence to study at Yale Law School, planning to return to the *Tribune* as legal editor.

A few days before my graduation, I settled into a cubicle in the law school's gothic library and unfolded the *New York Times* for a leisurely morning of reading. I was already prepared for my final exams and was getting excited about returning to Chicago.

Then my friend Howard appeared. I folded the newspaper and greeted him; he stared at me as if he had something urgent to say but couldn't find the right words. "What's wrong?" I asked. He didn't answer, but somehow I knew. "My father died, right?"

He nodded, then led me to the privacy of a small alcove, where I sobbed inconsolably.

Alone with My Father

Before my father's wake began at the funeral parlor, I asked for the room to be cleared. I stood in front of the open casket for the longest time. A lifetime of thoughts tumbled through my mind. My emotions churned. There was nothing to say, and yet there was everything to say.

So many times in my life, I had rationalized away my need to take responsibility for the role I had played in our relational breakdown. *He's the one who should be apologizing to me.* Or pride got in my way. *Why should I go crawling to him?* Or sometimes I'd just put it off. *I can always handle that later.*

Finally, after a long period of silence, I managed to whisper the words I desperately wished I had spoken so many years earlier: "I'm sorry, Dad."

Sorry for the ways I had rebelled against him, lied to him, and disrespected him over the years. Sorry for my ingratitude. Sorry for the bitterness and rancor I had allowed to poison my heart. For the first time, I admitted my own culpability in our relational strife.

Then came my last words to my father: "I forgive you." As best I could, I extended him grace—too late for our relationship, but in so many ways liberating and life-changing for me.

Over time, I found that nothing heals like grace.

Unexpected Words

Soon business associates, neighbors, golfing buddies, and others arrived at the wake to offer condolences to my mother and other family members. I sat by myself in a folding chair off to the side. I was dealing with deep and conflicted emotions and didn't feel like interacting with anyone.

One of my dad's business associates walked over and sat down beside me. "Are you Lee?" he asked.

"Yes, I am," I said. We shook hands.

"Well, it's great to finally meet you after hearing so much about you," he said. "Your dad could never stop talking about you. He was so proud of you and excited about what you're doing. Every time you'd have an article in the *Tribune*, he'd clip it and show it to everyone. When you went off to Yale—well, he was bursting with pride. He was always showing us pictures of your kids. He couldn't stop bragging about you. It's good to finally put a face with the name because we heard your name a lot from your dad. 'Lee's doing this.' 'Lee's doing that.' 'Did you see Lee's article on the front page?' But then, I suppose you knew all that."

My mind reeled as I tried to conceal my astonishment. I couldn't help wondering what might have been different if those words had come to me directly from my dad.

When I became a follower of Jesus several years later, I saw the stark contrast. Here, there was no concealing how my Father felt about me. In direct declarations, the Bible shouted over and over: *God's love for me is unrestrained and unconditional; his grace is lavish and unending. I am his workmanship and his pride, and he couldn't stand the thought of spending eternity without me in his family.*

And as God's grace utterly rocked my life — forgiving me, adopting me, and changing my life and my eternity — something else became clear: how tragic it would be to withhold the news of that grace from others. How could I revel in it myself but never pass it along to a world that is dying for it? As atheist Penn Jillette said, "How much do you have to hate somebody to believe that everlasting life is possible and not tell them that?"[1]

What if Michelle had never hugged Cody Huff? What if Luis Palau had never written his letters to his son Andrew? What if the woman in the refugee camp had never revealed the meaning of the cross to Christopher LaPel? As the apostle Paul asked, how can people believe in Christ if they have never heard about him?[2]

"[God] dispenses his goodness not with an eyedropper but a fire hydrant. Your heart is a Dixie cup and his grace is the Mediterranean Sea. You simply can't contain it all," said Max Lucado. "So let it bubble over. Spill out. Pour forth. 'Freely you have received, freely give.'"[3]

Writing about my journey of grace in this book has only strengthened my resolve to emulate the apostle Paul. "What matters most to me," Paul wrote, "is to finish what God started: the job the Master Jesus gave me of letting everyone I meet know all about this incredibly extravagant generosity of God."[4]

That is the joyful task of every follower of Jesus. Someday may it be written about me on my tombstone: *He was so amazed by God's grace that he couldn't keep it to himself.*

Discussion Guide

When a story intrigues, inspires, or challenges me, the first thing I like to do is discuss it with someone. I've found that I'm more likely to apply the lessons of a story if I'm in a circle of friends who each offer insights. In community, truth often goes deepest.

That's why I asked my friend Garry Poole, an award-winning author of numerous discussion guides, to help me create a series of questions that will encourage you to delve more deeply into the stories in this book. Yes, the questions can aid you in privately reflecting on what you've read, but my hope is you'll join with a few friends to grow together in your understanding and application of God's grace.

This is not a Bible study. Instead, it's designed to stimulate our thinking about grace and explore how it can change our lives and eternities. You'll quickly see that we have provided more questions than a group could go through in each session. We did this intentionally so that a leader can sift through them and select the ones that best fit the group.

Regardless of where you find yourself on your spiritual journey, we hope this guide will lead you into a more robust appreciation of God's grace and how it applies to your own circumstances. In the safety of authentic community, let's honestly dialogue so we can emerge ever more invigorated and transformed by the wonder of grace.

Preface, Introduction, and
CHAPTER 1: The Mistake

1. In your opinion, what makes a great father? What are the top three traits of a terrific dad?

2. When you hear the word "grace," what's the first image or thought that springs to mind? What does the term "grace" mean to you?

   Eugene O'Neill said that man is born broken and the grace of God is glue, and I think that's pretty true, that it's divine glue.... I experience it as buoyancy, as a very strange sense of calm in the midst of tremendous anxiety and lostness. I often get my sense of humor back, or I just feel safe and in God's care.   —ANNE LAMOTT

3. In her book *Sin Boldly*, Cathleen Falsani compares the concepts of justice, mercy, and grace this way:

   Justice is getting what you deserve.
   Mercy is not getting what you deserve.
   And grace is getting what you absolutely don't deserve.
   ... [It's] benign good will. Unprovoked compassion. The unearnable gift.

   Do you agree with these comparisons? Why or why not? Using a real-life example, can you illustrate the differences between justice, mercy, and grace?

4. Describe an occasion when you received or offered grace. What happened? How did the experience make you feel? What was the outcome?

5. Are you more apt to receive grace, extend grace, or neither? Explain your response. Why do you think this is true of you?

   Grace humbles us without degrading us and elevates us without inflating us.   —KEN BOA

6. What reservations do you have about discussing a book of stories about God's grace? What benefits do you anticipate gaining? How might the stories in this book help you to live out your own story of renewal by grace?

7. Here are some pieces to the grace puzzle:
    • forgiveness from God
    • forgiveness from others
    • forgiving others
    • forgiving ourselves
    • unconditional acceptance
    • adoption into God's family
    • hope for the future

   Which piece is most difficult for you to grasp? Which one is easiest to implement? Which one do you most need to experience in your life right now? Why?

8. The apostle Paul describes the benefits of receiving God's grace: "Therefore, since we have been justified through faith, we have peace with God through our Lord Jesus Christ, through whom we have gained access by faith into his grace in which we now stand. And we rejoice in the hope of the glory of God" (Romans 5:1–2). Imagine receiving grace from God. What would that look like to you? How might that experience impact you?

9. A. W. Tozer said: "[God] waits to be wanted. Too bad that with many of us He waits so long, so very long, in vain." Why do you think people resist God? What are some ways in which you have resisted God in the past? How resistant are you to God right now?

   Grace is God loving, God stooping, God coming to the rescue, God giving himself generously in and through Jesus Christ.
   —JOHN STOTT

10. How significant are words of affirmation, appreciation, and affection to children growing up? To what extent did you hear such words as a child? How were you impacted by hearing or not hearing them?

11. Where would you place yourself on the scale below? Where would your friends place you on the scale? Is there a discrepancy between the two? Give reasons for your responses.

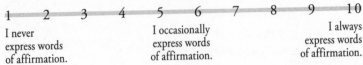

| 1 | 2 | 3 | 4 | 5 | 6 | 7 | 8 | 9 | 10 |

I never
express words
of affirmation.

I occasionally
express words
of affirmation.

I always
express words
of affirmation.

12. Lee describes a time when his dad inadvertently left him at the church. Lee may not have fully realized the impact of this incident at the time, but it became a vivid memory. What is one vivid memory you have of your relationship with your father? Why do you think that recollection lingers for you?

13. Describe your relationship with your father growing up. To what extent has that relationship influenced your concept of God? What are some other factors that have impacted your beliefs about God?

14. When Lee left home, he said he was on a mission fueled by rage. What was Lee's mission? What is *your* mission in life—and what do you think fuels it?

15. To what extent can you relate to Lee's confusion about spiritual matters? What spiritual issues most perplex you?

16. What's missing in your life?

17. Select a number on the scale below that best indicates where you are right now on your spiritual journey. Explain your response.

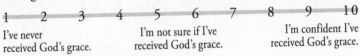

| 1 | 2 | 3 | 4 | 5 | 6 | 7 | 8 | 9 | 10 |

I've never
received God's grace.

I'm not sure if I've
received God's grace.

I'm confident I've
received God's grace.

18. In the original Greek, John 1:18 uses the idiom "in the bosom" to describe the closeness of God the Son and God the Father. In effect, says Michael Reeves in his book *Delighting in the Trinity*, John is painting a picture of Jesus as being eternally in the bosom or lap of the Father. "One would never dare imagine it," said Reeves, "but Jesus declares that his desire is that believers might be with him there (John 17:24)." For a moment, dare to picture yourself sitting securely in the lap of your gracious heavenly Father. What thoughts and emotions come to you? In what ways would this experience affect you?

CHAPTER 2: The Orphan

1. Describe your earliest childhood memory.

2. Storytelling gives us refreshing ways of viewing our past, our emotions, our hopes and dreams, our self-understanding, our purpose, and our world. What aspect of Stephanie Fast's story stands out in your mind? What had the most impact on you? Can you explain why?

3. Describe an experience when you or someone you know was left behind. What was the outcome? What emotions came into play?

4. When Stephanie was a young child, her mother put her on a train and gave her instructions to meet her uncle at one of the stops. She did as she was told, but no one came for her. What's your reaction to this part of her story? Describe the flood of emotions Stephanie (and her mother) must have experienced during this time. What do you suppose her mother's intentions were? Do you think there ever really was an uncle? Do you think Stephanie's mother ever tried to locate her daughter? Give reasons for your responses.

5. Stephanie's abandonment and homelessness, combined with the

endless taunting from others, left her with a poor self-image. She explains, "I was worthless. I was dirty. I was unclean. I had no name. I had no identity. I had no family. I had no future and no hope. Over time, I began to hate myself." What are some of the lasting repercussions or consequences of low self-esteem? To what extent can you relate to Stephanie's spiral of negative self-talk? If you feel comfortable, how would you describe your current level of self-worth?

> *The human heart is never changed through laws. It is changed*
> *through grace.*   —RICK WARREN

6. Names can have a huge influence on us. Stephanie began to think of herself as garbage, because of the name others had called her. If you feel comfortable sharing, what names were you called as a child that shaped your identity growing up?

7. Stephanie longed to belong. What do you long for? To what extent do you feel you belong? Where—and to whom—do you belong?

8. Stephanie recounts two haunting questions she had as a child: "Why am I so bad that people want to kill me? Why can't I be like other children who have a mommy and daddy?" Imagine if Stephanie had confronted you with these questions. How would you respond to her?

9. Describe one of your earliest memories of fatherly or motherly love. How did you react? How does that memory impact you today?

10. Lee describes the scene in the orphanage of an aspiring father bringing unconditional acceptance to an orphan who had absolutely nothing to offer, no accolades or accomplishments, just herself in all her vulnerability and scars and weaknesses. How is this image a glimpse of God's grace? What aspect of that scene resonates most with you personally?

11. Stephanie recounts how she rejected grace by spitting into the face of the man who reached out to her. How might you explain why she reacted in this way? What inner struggle was she facing? How have you rejected grace in the past? Are there ways in which you are rejecting grace now?

12. Given Stephanie's emotional baggage and physical ailments, and the level of sacrifice required to care for her, how do you explain why David and Judy Merwin selected her as the one to adopt?

13. When Stephanie was adopted by the Merwins, she could only make sense of it in terms of a transactional exchange: she would work her way out of her indebtedness to them. Why do you suppose this was Stephanie's initial reaction to being adopted? In what ways can you relate to this way of thinking? To what extent is the concept of grace counter-intuitive?

> *Wouldn't it be funny if God only cared about how you looked?*
>
> —COMEDIAN ALBERT BROOKS

14. Using the scale below, indicate your reaction to the grace that God offers you. Give reasons for your response.

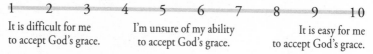

1	2	3	4	5	6	7	8	9	10
It is difficult for me to accept God's grace.				I'm unsure of my ability to accept God's grace.				It is easy for me to accept God's grace.	

15. Stephanie struggled with overwhelming feelings of shame, guilt, and inadequacy, which prevented her from believing God could love and accept her unconditionally. What barriers prevent you from believing God loves and accepts you unconditionally?

16. J. I. Packer writes, "Our understanding of Christianity cannot be better than our grasp of adoption.... Of all the gifts of grace, adoption is the highest." Explain what you think Packer meant. Do you agree with him? Why or why not?

17. Suppose Stephanie could somehow reconnect with her mother. What would be the first words each of them might say to the other? Do you believe Stephanie could offer her mother grace? Should she? Could you? Why or why not?

18. Stephanie's story offered insight into Lee's life: God not only erased his sins but became Lee's loving and compassionate Father, filling a heart left empty by an earthly dad. How does Stephanie's story affect your understanding of God's grace?

19. John 1:12 says, "Yet to all who received him, to those who believed in his name, he gave the right to become children of God. . . ." According to this verse, what two elements are involved in becoming God's child? How do they relate to you? To what extent do you currently view yourself as a child—a son, a daughter—of God? Please elaborate.

CHAPTER 3: The Addict

1. Even though what happens in Vegas is supposed to stay in Vegas, share something funny that happened when you, or someone you know, visited Las Vegas.

2. Jud's teenage years were focused on "escaping to freedom." What were you focused on as a teenager? How would your parents and friends have described you in those years? What's the biggest way in which you've changed since then?

3. What is the difference between an occasional mild obsession and an addictive one? What turns routine behavior into an addiction? Do you agree that some people appear to have an addictive nature and others seem immune from becoming ensnared by an addiction? Why or why not? To what extent are you prone to addiction?

4. Jud describes hitting bottom and realizing he was on the edge of everything coming unraveled. What, specifically, does this mean? To what extent can you relate?

5. At one low point in his life, Jud resigned himself into thinking, "I might die. And I'm okay with that." Why do you suppose he feared living more than dying? If you feel comfortable, share an era when you or someone you know no longer had the will to keep living. What was it that led to this place?

6. The Psalms contain some desperate cries to God. Psalm 88 begins: "LORD, you are the God who saves me; day and night I cry out to you. May my prayer come before you; turn your ear to my cry" (verses 1–2). Psalm 142:6 says: "Listen to my cry, for I am in desperate need...." At his darkest hour, Jud realized he "couldn't do it alone," and he called out to God for help. How difficult is it for you to admit you can't do life alone? Is there a time when you cried out to God for help? What happened?

7. After his prayer of desperation, Jud felt as if he had arrived at the place where he belonged. Where is this place? Describe it. To what extent are you at the place where you belong? Where is that place?

> *I rejected the church for a time because I found so little grace there. I returned because I found grace nowhere else.* —PHILIP YANCEY

8. Jud connected with a small community of Christians that quickly became a "safe place" for him. What does a "safe place" look like to you? In what ways have you experienced this kind of connection, acceptance, love, and safety in community? Have you found church to be a safe place for you? Why or why not?

9. What's the difference between "religion" and "faith"? How can religion be an obstacle for spiritual growth and discovery?

10. Jud jumped on the "performance treadmill" with a compulsion to prove he was good enough to deserve God's continuing love. What exactly is the performance trap? What are the dangers of living this way? What drives you toward being performance oriented? What determines the difference between healthy motivations and unhealthy ones?

11. Place an X on the number that most closely identifies where you are:

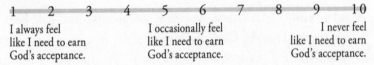

| 1 | 2 | 3 | 4 | 5 | 6 | 7 | 8 | 9 | 10 |

I always feel like I need to earn God's acceptance.   I occasionally feel like I need to earn God's acceptance.   I never feel like I need to earn God's acceptance.

12. Tullian Tchividjian, in his book *One Way Love*, said: "It often seems that the Good News of God's grace has been tragically hijacked by an oppressive religious moralism that is all about rules, rules, and more rules. Doing more, trying harder, self-help, getting better, and fixing, fixing, fixing — ourselves, our kids, our spouses, our friends, our enemies, our culture, our world. Christianity is perceived as being a vehicle for good behavior and clean living — and the judgments that result from them — rather than the only recourse for those who have failed over and over and over again." Do you agree with his assessment? Have you seen this tendency in churches? What about in your own life?

13. How much can you identify with this statement: "I knew that I was saved by God's grace alone, but now I was trying to earn my keep. Jesus had paid my debt, but I felt like I needed to repay him."

14. Jud said, "After I rediscovered the beauty of grace, I began to relax in my faith. I started to enjoy God again instead of feeling like I had to prove something to him." What does it mean to relax in one's faith? To what extent do you feel like you need to relax more in your faith? What would that look like in your life?

15. What expectations of yourself and others do you carry around with you? What expectations does God place on you? Whose expectations put the most pressure on you: God, others, or you? How do these expectations make you feel?

16. What is religious legalism? Ken Blue says in *The Gospel Uncensored* that it's "the belief that you can or must add any human effort to the work of Christ." What are the dangers and symptoms of it? What has been your experience with legalism? How does one find the healthy balance between unhealthy legalism and healthy goals and expectations?

    > *We would like to think that Jesus said, "Well done, my highly productive servant."*
    > —KENNY LUCK

17. Do you agree that people who are filled with guilt, shame, and brokenness have a difficult time allowing God's grace to sink in? Why or why not? To what extent do people who do not carry around guilt, shame, and brokenness have a difficult time receiving God's grace? What about you? To what degree do you carry around guilt, shame, and brokenness? How difficult is it for you to fully embrace God's grace?

18. Are you apt to give people the benefit of the doubt? Why or why not? What are the benefits of giving people the benefit of the doubt? Any downsides?

19. What's your assessment: Do most Christians hate the sin *and* the sinner? Explain your response. What about you? To what extent do you hate the sin and love the sinner? What are the obstacles in doing that?

    > *Christianity is not a religion; it is the announcement of the end of religion.*
    > —ROBERT CAPON

20. Jud sees grace and truth as two sides of the same coin. What do you think he meant by this? Do you agree or disagree? Why?

21. "Where sin increased, grace increased all the more" (Romans 5:20). How do you interpret this verse? How does this verse relate to your experience? Are you more aware of your failings or God's forgiveness? Why?

CHAPTER 4: *The Professor*

1. As a teenager, Craig Hazen liked to learn. How much of a learner are you? Which learning method do you prefer: reading, listening, observing, or doing? Why?

2. Visiting a church one evening, Hazen decided to put God to the test by becoming a Christian. What's your reaction to his "grand experiment"? What would he have to lose? What might he gain? Have you ever done anything similar?

3. Which is more difficult: a relatively good, moral person receiving God's grace, or an evil person doing so? Explain your reasoning. What would the pathway look like for these two kinds of people? What are the similarities and the differences? How would you help an average, law abiding, benevolent, good person recognize their need for grace?

   Sin is not a regrettable lapse or an occasional stumble. Sin stages a coup against God's regime.   —MAX LUCADO

4. Why do you think there are so many different religions in the world? Do you think all religions are basically the same? Why or why not? How has this chapter influenced your thinking on this topic?

5. Craig Hazen illustrates the difference between mercy and grace

this way: Suppose a parent discovers a child doing something wrong. Mercy is not punishing the child, while grace is giving the child a gift. In Christianity, God not only does not punish followers of Jesus, but he rewards them with complete forgiveness and eternal life as a gift. What do you think of Hazen's analogy? Do you agree that it depicts God's offerings of mercy and grace accurately? Why or why not?

6. Hazen said: "That's what grace is—an amazing gift that we don't deserve and cannot earn or contribute to. It's lavish, it's undeserved, it's extravagant—it's unmerited favor that God bestows freely to those willing to receive it. We can't earn it, we can't contribute to it, we can't repay him for it, we can't take any credit for it, but God offers it because he made us in his image and he wants to have a relationship with us for eternity. That's the Good News of the gospel." What is your reaction to this concept of God's grace? What do you like and dislike about it? What's the hardest aspect of it to understand—or to embrace?

7. How would you define "sin"? What does Hazen mean when he suggests that society has "lost the concept of sin"? Do you agree with him? Why or why not? How do you reconcile this view of society with Jud Wilhite's comment that he "rarely has to convince people that sin exists" in Las Vegas?

8. Do you agree or disagree with the Bible's teachings that no one is truly good (Romans 3:23)? Why? To what extent do you suppose your friends and family members view themselves as sinners? What about you?

9. Hazen said the self-esteem movement has contributed to our lack of understanding of the holiness of God and the depth of our sinfulness. Is it possible to have both a healthy perception of one's sin

and a healthy self-esteem, or are the two mutually exclusive? Why or why not?

> *What the world needs, I am ashamed to say, is Christian love.*
> —ATHEIST BERTRAND RUSSELL

10. Hazen contends that a clear understanding of grace starts with a clear understanding of sin. How does the awareness of one's sin contribute to a fuller, more robust appreciation of grace?

11. To what extent is unconditional love possible? Have you experienced it in your own life? Can you give an example?

12. According to Christianity, an accurate understanding of one's standing before God can evoke two strong reactions: Sheer horror at the magnitude of the separation from God caused by sin or overwhelming gratitude and joy for the gift of forgiveness and eternal life provided by God's grace. How much can you identify with these two positions?

13. Imagine a salesman facing termination if he doesn't meet his quota but never being told what the quota is. How would he or she feel? In a similar way, how would a system of having to earn our way to God lead to a terrible state of anxiety?

14. Theologian Russell D. Moore said, "Some people are deceived into thinking they are too good for the gospel while others are accused into thinking they're too bad for the gospel." Which category are you more apt to fall into and why? How about most of the people you know?

15. Describe encounters you have had in the past with members of other faiths outside of Christianity. What aspects of those religions appeal to you? What don't you like about them? Where do you disagree with their teachings? How do other faiths tend to be built around doing good works?

16. In *Unveiling Grace*, Lynn K. Wilder describes her frustration as a Mormon when she tried to "earn brownie points" by performing good works to earn God's favor. "All day long, I worried, perhaps not consciously but unconsciously, if what *I* was doing was the right thing. I worried whether each decision *I* was making throughout the day was moving *me* closer to being good enough to be accepted by Heavenly Father.... I did not realize that constantly evaluating my own righteousness was self-centered.... I was thinking about *me* all the time. Plus, I gave myself credit for being able to stave off sin. This groundless belief was toxic to my soul, blinding me to the many sins I *did* have." Wilder ended up leaving the Mormon faith. What do you think of her critique of a works-based faith? How does grace change our attitude toward ourselves — and God?

17. Hazen said that Christianity's uniqueness among the world religions is the gift of grace, with its commitment to the holiness of a personal God, the reality of sin, and its overarching historical grounding. How would you explain the uniqueness of Christianity to someone who has not yet crossed the line of faith? What would you emphasize and why?

    For grace is given not because we have done good works, but in order that we may be able to do them. —AUGUSTINE

18. To what extent do you agree with the following: "Grace opens the door to a relationship with God through no merit of our own, and yet it's merely wishful thinking unless Christianity is based on truth"? Explain your response.

19. Experiences, feelings, historical facts, logic, and truth can all influence our faith. What role has each of these factors played in your own spiritual journey? Which of these factors have you put to the "test"? Explain.

20. First John 5:13 says, "I write these things to you who believe in the Son of God so that you may know you have eternal life." On a scale from 1 to 10, how confident are you that you have eternal life? What would it take for you to move closer to a 10 on the scale?

CHAPTER FIVE: The Executioner

1. As a child, Christopher LaPel cherished a small ivory cross he wore around his neck. What religious item or article, if any, did you cherish growing up? Why did it mean so much to you, and whatever became of it?

2. To encourage him to discard the cross, LaPel's father offered to make any idol he wanted. But Christopher wished to continue to wear the cross. In what ways have you been encouraged to discontinue your spiritual quest for truth? How have you maintained your resolve in spite of the obstacles?

3. C. S. Lewis wrote, "To be a Christian means to forgive the inexcusable, because God has forgiven the inexcusable in you." Do you agree with the Christian concept of forgiving others as much as God has forgiven us? Why or why not?

4. On a scale from 1 to 10, how willing are you to forgive others?

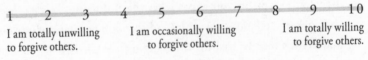

| 1 | 2 | 3 | 4 | 5 | 6 | 7 | 8 | 9 | 10 |

I am totally unwilling to forgive others.   I am occasionally willing to forgive others.   I am totally willing to forgive others.

5. Do you believe there are limits to God's grace? If so, where does he draw the line? If not, why not?

> *Forgiveness may be unfair—it is, by definition—but at least it provides a way to halt the juggernaut of retribution.*
>
> —PHILIP YANCEY

6. Describe a time when you, or someone you know, escaped a near-death or near-tragic experience. How did that impact you or your friend's attitude toward God? What promises were made? Did they become broken promises? Please elaborate.

7. LaPel decided to commit his life to God as a result of being spared from certain death. What's your reaction to "death-bed conversions"? Are they real? Sincere? Long-lasting? Why or why not?

8. When is turning to God at the point of desperation a form of escapism or, in Bonhoeffer's words, "cheap grace"? Is it possible to give mere lip service to Jesus in order to get a "ticket" to heaven? What's the difference between being an admirer of Jesus Christ and a devoted follower of him?

9. LaPel decided to give his life completely to God, vowing to devote himself to serving him no matter what. To what extent have you (or have you not) given your life to God? How satisfied are you with your current level of devotion to God? What would it take for you to give 100 percent to him?

10. Anticipating his own arrest and imprisonment, Duch said, "It is okay. They have my body. Jesus has my soul." What does this mean? Where did this confidence come from? To what extent would you like to be able to say the same thing?

11. If you were one of the few S-21 survivors, how difficult would it be for you to forgive Duch? Do you think you could eventually forgive him? How is forgiving him "fair"?

12. Read the parable of the unmerciful servant in Matthew 18:21–35. What's your reaction? What does it teach about forgiving others? Biblically speaking, is it possible to truly receive God's forgiveness and yet not forgive others? Why or why not?

13. If you were in LaPel's shoes and going to face Duch in his prison for the first time, what would you say to him? How would you act toward him?

14. How do you explain Duch's statement from inside the walls of prison, "I'm not a prisoner; I'm a free man." Jesus said in John 8:36, "So if the Son sets you free, you will be free indeed." What do you think he meant by that?

15. What's your opinion: was Duch's conversion authentic? Why or why not? What are some clues concerning whether someone has really put their trust in Christ? How many of those clues would others see in your own life?

> Be kind and compassionate to one another, forgiving each other, just as in Christ God forgave you.   —EPHESIANS 4:32

16. How do you respond to Herbert Marcuse's statement: "One cannot, and should not go around happily killing and torturing and then, when the moment has come, simply ask, and receive, forgiveness." How could God possibly offer forgiveness and eternal life to a person who commits heinous criminal acts like Pol Pot, the "Hitler of Cambodia," if he merely asks for forgiveness? Doesn't that cheapen grace—or does it make it all the more amazing? Explain your thinking.

17. Do you agree with this statement: "If Jesus is really the only way to salvation, then his Buddhist victims would go to hell, but Duch would spend eternity in heaven." Why or why not? How do you make sense of this?

18. Do you agree or disagree: "If some sins are unforgiveable, then Jesus's mission fell short." Why or why not?

19. To what extent do you believe you are completely forgiven by God, and yet still carry remorse for your sins? Do you live with regret? To what extent? Why?

CHAPTER SIX: The Homeless

1. What most impacted you about Cody Huff's story? Why?

2. Philip Yancey wrote, "Grace means there is nothing we can do to make God love us more ... and there is nothing we can do to make God love us less." If this is true, what does this say about God's love? Do you *really* believe that there is nothing you could do to make God love you less? Explain.

3. Describe a time when you prayed, "God, why are you doing this to me?"

4. Cody Huff reached the point where every ounce of his dignity was gone. What does it mean to lose one's dignity? He goes on to say, "I hated myself. I hated my life—and I hated God." What precipitated this hatred toward himself and God? To what extent can you relate to Huff's hatred of himself?

In loving your neighbor, it's the small gestures that make the biggest impact.
—ED STETZER

5. When were you at the lowest point in your life, when you felt like your life was in a tailspin, and how did you react? In anger? In prayer? In tears? In self-medication? In disbelief? In denial? In depression? What did you learn from this experience?

6. Honestly, from where do you gain your sense of identity or self-worth (family, friends, job, physical appearance, talents and abilities, finances, and so on)? Elaborate on your answer. Someone once said our self-esteem is based on what we think the most important person in our life thinks about us. Who is most important in your life—and what does he or she think about you?

7. Cody Huff said, "I *had* nothing, and I *was* nothing." Imagine that this was you, stripped of your identity and self-worth. Also, imagine you have no bed or home. What does this feel like? How would

you react? What would you have done differently than Cody if you were in his situation?

8. Why couldn't Cody break the cycle he found himself in: the pattern of self-preservation, then self-destruction; gaining everything, then losing everything; getting off drugs, then getting hooked again; finding a legitimate job, then falling back into crime? What do you think causes this pattern in people? To what degree can you relate to being stuck in an unproductive cycle?

9. Do you believe it's possible to break destructive patterns without God? Why or why not?

10. What has been your experience with the homeless? What is your unvarnished initial reaction when you see a beggar on the street? Have you or someone you know ever volunteered to serve in a homeless shelter? What was the experience like and what feelings surfaced?

11. Do you have a strategy for how you handle being approached by a homeless person asking for money? Do you think you should give him or her money, certificates for food, or nothing? Why or why not? How big of a problem is homelessness in your community? How would your church react if the pastor decided to allow the homeless to sleep there?

12. Why do you think Michelle gave Cody a hug when he was dirty, smelly, and homeless? If you were in Michelle's shoes, would you have shaken Cody's hand, given him a bear hug or even a pat on the back? Why or why not? Do you believe a simple, kind gesture can break a lifetime cycle of self-destruction? What are two or three ways you could embody God's love to someone else?

13. How would you answer Max Lucado's question: "How long has it been since your generosity stunned someone?"

14. Gary Chapman's book *The Five Love Languages* identifies different ways of expressing love: gifts, quality time, words of affirmation, acts of service, and physical touch. How can grace be expressed using this rubric? How do you typically express grace?

15. In the moment of Heather's hug, something spiritual sparked inside of Cody, and yet, even to this day, he is unable to articulate exactly what occurred. How would you explain what happened at that instant? Have you ever experienced anything like that?

16. Cody likens Michelle's gesture to a personal encounter with Jesus, as if Jesus himself were standing in front of him. Do you believe God uses people to "stand in" for Jesus? Have you ever been used like this? Has someone "been Jesus" to you? How so?

> *If you are renewed by grace, and were to meet your old self, I am sure you would be very anxious to get out of his company.*
>
> —CHARLES SPURGEON

17. Some people experience instant transformation after crying out to God; others reach out to God and do not seem to be changed in the least. Why do you think there is such a wide spectrum of experiences in this regard?

18. Cody revealed how everything culminated for him at the park he called home. "I didn't really know anything about the Bible, except God loves me, Jesus died for me, I'm a sinner, forgiveness is available — and I wanted it." How well does this statement summarize the gospel? To what degree do you believe what Cody believed — and want what Cody wanted?

19. Cody described how he was consumed by an incredible sense of peace when he prayed to receive God's forgiveness and grace. He said, "It was like a wave in the ocean, like when I was surfing and a wave would *whoosh* over me. I felt clean for the first time." Do

you need what Cody received? How much would you like to feel the sense of cleansing Cody experienced? Describe the last time you prayed a heartfelt prayer.

21. How has your understanding of grace developed since you started reading this book? Are you more or less apt to receive God's grace? How are you more or less likely to extend God's grace to others? Explain.

CHAPTER SEVEN: The Pastor

1. In 41 percent of marriages, one or both spouses admit to physical or emotional cheating. Why do you think infidelity has become commonplace in our society? What are the biggest effects of this phenomenon?

2. Brennan Manning said, "To live by grace means to acknowledge my whole life story, the light side and the dark. In admitting my shadow side I learn who I am and what God's grace means." Using a scale from 1 to 10, how aware are you of your shadow side? On a scale from 1 to 10, how willing are you to acknowledge your shadow side to trusted friends or family members? Elaborate.

3. Which is more gut-wrenching: the agony of being the victim of betrayal or the remorse, regret, and guilt of being the perpetrator of betrayal? Why? Which is more difficult: a husband or wife extending grace and forgiveness to an unfaithful spouse, or an unfaithful spouse receiving grace and forgiving himself or herself? Explain.

   How shalt thou hope for mercy, rendering none?
   —SHAKESPEARE, *THE MERCHANT OF VENICE*

4. Heidi is more of a peacemaker; Brad is more of a peacekeeper. What's the difference? To what degree are you a peacemaker or a peacekeeper?

5. Brad said he is a people-pleaser. What does this mean? Is this a negative or positive trait? Why? How much are you a people-pleaser?

6. C. S. Lewis wrote, "Pride is the mother hen under which all other sins are hatched." Do you agree with him? Why or why not? Proverbs 16:18 says, "Pride goes before destruction, a haughty spirit before a fall." In what ways is that true?

7. Brad struggled with entitlement issues. What does this entail, and what are the dangers associated with this attitude? Have you struggled with the same thing? If you are willing, share an example.

8. Brad said that "even on the way to the first encounter," he knew he should turn around. Why do you think he didn't? Have you ever proceeded to do something that you knew in your heart was the wrong thing to do?

9. To what extent should people trust others? To what extent do you trust others? To what extent do you trust yourself? What process do you think is required in order for people to reestablish trust when trust has been broken?

> *Guilt was not my problem as I felt it. What I felt most was a glob of unworthiness that I could not tie down to any concrete sins I was guilty of. What I needed more than pardon was a sense that God accepted me, owned me, held me, affirmed me, and would never let go of me even if he was not too much impressed with what he had on his hands.* —LEWIS SMEDES

10. What is your reaction to this verse: "Do not be deceived: God cannot be mocked" (Galatians 6:7). How might this apply to your life?

11. Unhealthy thinking (entitlement beliefs, lack of trusting God, pride, defensiveness) plus hurtful feelings (underappreciated, not enough validation from others, job frustration, bitterness,

deserving better) coupled with circumstances (long distance com-
muting, not connecting with Heidi in honest communication,
a woman needing help with her Bible study) all contributed to
Brad's downfall. In seeking to learn from Brad's experience, what
are some of the warning flags you and others should heed?

12. Brad describes "living a charade." How have you felt the internal
tension of leading a duplicitous life? How heavy was the "weight"
for you? Describe.

13. What explanation can you give for how Brad and Heidi moved
from hurt to healing? To what extent is this pathway possible for
others going through a similar hardship? What attitudes are necessary for this to happen? Explain.

14. Heidi decided to forgive Brad without first feeling the forgiveness.
How do you explain this? What conclusions can you draw regard-
ing Heidi's character that she would choose to forgive Brad? Could
you imagine doing the same thing? Why or why not?

15. Is it possible (or necessary) to forgive someone who is unwilling
to admit or apologize for his or her wrongdoing? Should we forgive people even if they are not sorry about how they harmed us?
Explain. We're told in Scripture to forgive as God forgives, and
he calls for repentance (Acts 3:19). How should this guide our
attitudes toward each other? What happens in our own lives when
we forgive unrepentant people?

16. Brad was broken and repentant. He also felt he needed to stand up
in front of the congregation and admit his sin in order to accept
complete responsibility so he could feel fully forgiven by God. Do
you agree that accepting full responsibility is tied to feeling fully
forgiven by God? Why or why not? Is public confession always
part of the process of accepting responsibility? Explain.

17. Define shame. Do you agree with Brad that shame is not from God? Why or why not? Are there any benefits to shame? If so, what are they?

18. Even though Brad knew that both God and Heidi had forgiven him, he had difficulty escaping feelings of shame and self-condemnation. How do you explain this? Why is grace elusive to people mired in sin and filled with shame? Why is it so hard to apply Romans 8:1 to ourselves: "Therefore, there is now no condemnation for those who are in Christ Jesus."

19. What are the depths you would go to forgive? Or is there a line that could be crossed which would be "too far" for you to forgive someone? Explain.

20. What's your reaction to Heidi's statement: "I never would have chosen it, but God used that experience to draw me closer to him than ever before." Has God used negative experiences in your life to create something good? How so?

CHAPTER EIGHT: The Prodigal

1. Do you pray? What does your prayer life look like? To what extent do your prayers get answered? How do you deal with seemingly unanswered prayer?

2. Andrew Palau put up a Christian front to mask his indifference toward anything spiritual. Do you suspect this is common among many who call themselves Christian? Why? What drives people to live lives of duplicity? Are there ways in which you have constructed a façade in your own life?

3. What does it mean to "worship at the altar of self"? To what extent is this something you've done?

4. How does the book of Proverbs describe a "fool"? Do you see any tendency in yourself toward any of these behaviors? How so?

> *We cannot find Him unless we know we need Him.*
>
> —THOMAS MERTON

5. Have you experienced a period in your life when you were fool-hardy, frivolous, selfish, apathetic toward spiritual matters, or bent on taking a wayward path? What was that like? What deterred you from that path?

6. Andrew turned from his Christian heritage. What prompts a child to spurn the values of their parents? To what extent are parents responsible for their children when it comes to spiritual matters?

7. Andrew grew up believing Christianity was true, but he didn't care. He said he loved his sin too much. Do you think Andrew really did think Christianity was true? Is it possible to intellectually agree with the tenets of Christianity but be apathetic toward the faith? In what ways can you relate to Andrew's attitude?

8. Andrew's father wrote a loving yet challenging letter to him. What was his basic message? How would you have reacted if you were in Andrew's shoes? Is there someone you need to write a similar letter to? Explain.

> *The entrance into the kingdom of God is through the sharp, sudden pains of repentance colliding with man's respectable "goodness."*
>
> —OSWALD CHAMBERS

9. Luis Palau wrote, "You were born, Andrew, to be a man of God." Do you believe that every person's purpose in life is to be a man or woman of God? Why or why not? To what extent do you think of yourself as a man or woman of God? How does this affect your mission in life?

10. Did anyone ever confront or challenge you to change the direction of your life? What were the circumstances? How did you receive it? What was the outcome?

11. To what degree can you relate to Andrew's haunting memories of hurting, using, or deceiving others? If you feel comfortable, share a memory that still bothers you.

12. What's your assessment of what happened when Andrew was asked if he was a follower of Satan? What do you suppose this person saw in Andrew that made him think he was devoted to the devil? Do you believe this was some sort of supernatural encounter or something else? Explain your response.

13. While visiting friends in Jamaica, Andrew became intrigued by people who were living the abundant life in a "winsome and radical" way. What do you suppose this kind of faith looked like? Describe a time when you were impressed in a similar way. What were the distinguishing traits and characteristics that set these Christians apart?

14. Why do people tend to do the very things they don't wish to do, and don't do the very things they do wish to do? Can you relate to this pattern? How so?

15. Andrew raised some tough questions when his life began to spiral out of control again: *How could I have been so sincere and yet fail so badly? And what was I supposed to do now?* How would you have responded to these two questions if you had been with him at the time?

> *I am always going into the far country, and always returning home as a prodigal, always saying Father, forgive me, and thou art always bringing forth the best robe.*   —PURITAN PRAYER

16. Andrew concluded that a salvation prayer doesn't mean much unless you authentically turn from sin and allow God to take over your life. Summarize what you think this means. Do you agree or disagree with Andrew's conclusion? Explain.

17. At one point, Andrew became frustrated because he wasn't able to understand what he was reading in the Bible. Do you read the Bible on a regular basis? Can you relate to Andrew's experience? What passage has particularly confounded you? What are some ways you might get answers to your questions about it?

18. What do you think it takes to personally experience God in one's life? What is your level of interest in relating to God in an intimate way? Explain your response.

19. Andrew's prayer focus shifted from "God, reveal yourself to me" to "God, what is keeping me from you?" What is the significant difference in this shift? What was keeping Andrew from God? What might be keeping you from God?

    God rejoices. Not because the problems of the world have been solved, not because all human pain and suffering have come to an end, nor because thousands of people have been converted and are now praising him for his goodness. No, God rejoices because one of his children who was lost has been found. —HENRI NOUWEN

20. Andrew said: "Repentance is the rebel's only path to God." Acts 3:19 says, "Repent, then, and turn to God, so that your sins may be wiped out, that times of refreshment may come from the Lord." How do you define repentance? Is it more than just feeling sorry for what you've done?

21. Andrew arrived at the place where he was able to sincerely admit he was wrong and God was right; to see his depravity clearly in contrast to God's holiness; and to receive God's cleansing and leadership of his life. Considering this description, where are you

in your spiritual journey? What are the barriers preventing you from taking another step toward God?

CHAPTER NINE: Empty Hands and the Epilogue

1. What impacted you most as you read Lee's story? Please explain.

2. Have you, or someone you know, ever experienced mental confusion, delusions, or hallucinations? Briefly explain the circumstances. How did you, your friends, and family react? What did you learn through that process?

3. At one point, Lee felt as though he was descending into hell. What do you believe, and not believe, about hell? What do you think the Bible teaches about it?

4. What positive outcomes resulted from Lee's visions of homelessness, bankruptcy, abandonment, and rejection?

5. In his confusion, Lee began to think that even Jesus had abandoned him. Have you ever felt that Jesus had abandoned you? What were the circumstances?

6. Lee's son, Kyle, offered a simple suggestion: "Dad, we need to pray." Describe a time when someone offered to pray with you. When was the last time you made that same suggestion to someone? Elaborate.

7. Do you agree that when we approach God, we tend to subconsciously hide who we really are in order to project an image that we're in control? Why or why not? What does it take to strip away that false self?

8. What impact would it have on your life if you sincerely prayed a prayer of surrender to God, similar to Lee's prayer? Would you be willing to try it?

9. What does it mean to "empty oneself" of one's identity? What is your soul's true identity?

> *Define yourself radically as one beloved by God. This is the true self. Every other identity is an illusion.*   —BRENNAN MANNING

10. What amazes you the most about God's grace? Do you agree that nothing liberates and heals like grace? Why or why not?

11. If your life had a theme song, what would it be and why?

12. Why do you suppose Lee and his father never discussed the incident that prompted Lee to leave home? What were some of the excuses Lee gave himself to avoid this heart-to-heart conversation? Are there ways you can relate to this?

13. Lee expressed regret for not taking responsibility for the role he played in the relational breakdown with his father. What unresolved issue are you refusing to address with someone? What's holding you back?

> *When you forgive someone, you slice away the wrong from the person who did it. You disengage that person from his hurtful act. You recreate him. At one moment you identify him ineradicably as the person who did you wrong. The next moment you change that identity. He is remade in your memory.*   —LEWIS SMEDES

14. Do you agree that the declarations in the Bible are a direct expression of how God feels about people—including you? Why or why not? What declarations by God register the deepest for you?

> *If grace is so amazing, why don't Christians show more of it?*
> —PHILIP YANCEY

15. How much can you relate to Lee's vision for his life: To be so amazed by God's grace that he can't keep it to himself? What are some practical ways you can let others know about the Good News of God's grace?

16. What do you want written on your tombstone? Can you put it in a sentence or two?

17. Specifically, in what ways have the stories of grace in this book inspired or motivated you?

18. Remember the verse from earlier in the book: "Yet to all who received him, to those who believed in his name, he gave the right to become children of God...." Its key words form an equation for how to become God's child: Believe + Receive = Become. Do you *believe* Jesus is the unique Son of God who died as your substitute to pay the penalty you deserved for your sins? If so, have you *received* his free gift of forgiveness and eternal life? If not, what is holding you back from receiving his grace right now through a prayer of repentance and faith? "If we confess our sins, he is faithful and just and will forgive us our sins and purify us from all unrighteousness" (1 John 1:9).

What the Bible Says About Grace

And I will pour out on the house of David and the inhabitants of Jerusalem a spirit of grace and supplication. They will look on me, the one they have pierced, and they will mourn for him as one mourns for an only child, and grieve bitterly for him as one grieves for a firstborn son.

—ZECHARIAH 12:10

And the child [Jesus] grew and became strong; he was filled with wisdom, and the grace of God was on him. —LUKE 2:40

The Word became flesh and made his dwelling among us. We have seen his glory, the glory of the one and only Son, who came from the Father, full of grace and truth. —JOHN 1:14

Out of his fullness we have all received grace in place of grace already given. —JOHN 1:16

For the law was given through Moses; grace and truth came through Jesus Christ. —JOHN 1:17

Now Stephen, a man full of God's grace and power, performed great wonders and signs among the people. —ACTS 6:8

When he arrived and saw what the grace of God had done, he was glad and encouraged them all to remain true to the Lord with all their hearts. —ACTS 11:23

When the congregation was dismissed, many of the Jews and devout converts to Judaism followed Paul and Barnabas, who talked with them and urged them to continue in the grace of God. —ACTS 13:43

So Paul and Barnabas spent considerable time there, speaking boldly for the Lord, who confirmed the message of his grace by enabling them to perform signs and wonders. —ACTS 14:3

We believe it is through the grace of our Lord Jesus that we are saved, just as they are. —ACTS 15:11

When Apollos wanted to go to Achaia, the brothers and sisters encouraged him and wrote to the disciples there to welcome him. When he arrived, he was a great help to those who by grace had believed. —ACTS 18:27

However, I consider my life worth nothing to me; my only aim is to finish the race and complete the task the Lord Jesus has given me—the task of testifying to the good news of God's grace. —ACTS 20:24

Now I commit you to God and to the word of his grace, which can build you up and give you an inheritance among all those who are sanctified. —ACTS 20:32

Through him we received grace and apostleship to call all the Gentiles to the obedience that comes from faith for his name's sake. —ROMANS 1:5

To all in Rome who are loved by God and called to be his holy people: Grace and peace to you from God our Father and from the Lord Jesus Christ. —ROMANS 1:7

And all are justified freely by his grace through the redemption that came by Christ Jesus. —ROMANS 3:24

Therefore, the promise comes by faith, so that it may be by grace and may be guaranteed to all Abraham's offspring—not only to those who are of the law but also to those who have the faith of Abraham. He is the father of us all. —ROMANS 4:16

But the gift is not like the trespass. For if the many died by the trespass of the one man, how much more did God's grace and the gift that came by the grace of the one man, Jesus Christ, overflow to the many! Nor can the gift of God be compared with the result of one man's sin: The judgment followed one sin and brought condemnation, but the gift followed many trespasses and brought justification. For if, by the trespass of the one man, death reigned through that one man, how much more will those who receive God's abundant provision of grace and of the gift of righteousness reign in life through the one man, Jesus Christ!   —ROMANS 5:15–17

The law was brought in so that the trespass might increase. But where sin increased, grace increased all the more, so that, just as sin reigned in death, so also grace might reign through righteousness to bring eternal life through Jesus Christ our Lord.   —ROMANS 5:20–21

What shall we say, then? Shall we go on sinning so that grace may increase? By no means! We are those who have died to sin; how can we live in it any longer? Or don't you know that all of us who were baptized into Christ Jesus were baptized into his death?   —ROMANS 6:1–3

For sin shall no longer be your master, because you are not under the law, but under grace. What then? Shall we sin because we are not under the law but under grace? By no means!   —ROMANS 6:14–15

So too, at the present time there is a remnant chosen by grace. And if by grace, then it cannot be based on works; if it were, grace would no longer be grace.
                                                                              —ROMANS 11:5–6

For by the grace given me I say to every one of you: Do not think of yourself more highly than you ought, but rather think of yourself with sober judgment, in accordance with the faith God has distributed to each of you.
                                                                              —ROMANS 12:3

We have different gifts, according to the grace given to each of us.
                                                                              —ROMANS 12:6

The God of peace will soon crush Satan under your feet. The grace of our Lord Jesus be with you.   —ROMANS 16:20

I always thank my God for you because of his grace given you in Christ Jesus.   —1 CORINTHIANS 1:4

By the grace God has given me, I laid a foundation as a wise builder, and someone else is building on it. But each one should build with care.   —1 CORINTHIANS 3:10

But by the grace of God I am what I am, and his grace to me was not without effect. No, I worked harder than all of them—yet not I, but the grace of God that was with me.   —1 CORINTHIANS 15:10

Now this is our boast: Our conscience testifies that we have conducted ourselves in the world, and especially in our relations with you, with integrity and godly sincerity. We have done so, relying not on worldly wisdom but on God's grace.   —2 CORINTHIANS 1:12

All this is for your benefit, so that the grace that is reaching more and more people may cause thanksgiving to overflow to the glory of God.   —2 CORINTHIANS 4:15

As God's co-workers we urge you not to receive God's grace in vain.   —2 CORINTHIANS 6:1

But since you excel in everything—in faith, in speech, in knowledge, in complete earnestness and in the love we have kindled in you—see that you also excel in this grace of giving.   —2 CORINTHIANS 8:7

For you know the grace of our Lord Jesus Christ, that though he was rich, yet for your sake he became poor, so that you through his poverty might become rich.   —2 CORINTHIANS 8:9

And in their prayers for you their hearts will go out to you, because of the surpassing grace God has given you.   —2 CORINTHIANS 9:14

But he said to me, "My grace is sufficient for you, for my power is made perfect in weakness." Therefore I will boast all the more gladly about my weaknesses, so that Christ's power may rest on me. —2 CORINTHIANS 12:9

I am astonished that you are so quickly deserting the one who called you to live in the grace of Christ and are turning to a different gospel—which is really no gospel at all. Evidently some people are throwing you into confusion and are trying to pervert the gospel of Christ. —GALATIANS 1:6–7

James, Cephas, and John, those esteemed as pillars, gave me and Barnabas the right hand of fellowship when they recognized the grace given to me. They agreed that we should go to the Gentiles, and they to the circumcised. —GALATIANS 2:9

I do not set aside the grace of God, for if righteousness could be gained through the law, Christ died for nothing! —GALATIANS 2:21

You who are trying to be justified by the law have been alienated from Christ; you have fallen away from grace. —GALATIANS 5:4

For he chose us in him before the creation of the world to be holy and blameless in his sight. In love he predestined us for adoption to sonship through Jesus Christ, in accordance with his pleasure and will—to the praise of his glorious grace, which he has freely given us in the One he loves. In him we have redemption through his blood, the forgiveness of sins, in accordance with the riches of God's grace that he lavished on us. —EPHESIANS 1:4–8

But because of his great love for us, God, who is rich in mercy, made us alive with Christ even when we were dead in transgressions—it is by grace you have been saved. And God raised us up with Christ and seated us with him in the heavenly realms in Christ Jesus, in order that in the coming ages he might show the incomparable riches of his grace, expressed in his kindness to us in Christ Jesus. For it is by grace you have been saved, through faith—and this is not from yourselves, it is the gift of God—not by works, so that no one can boast. —EPHESIANS 2:4–9

*I became a servant of this gospel by the gift of God's grace given me through
the working of his power. Although I am less than the least of all the Lord's
people, this grace was given me: to preach to the Gentiles the boundless riches
of Christ, and to make plain to everyone the administration of this mystery,
which for ages past was kept hidden in God, who created all things.*

—EPHESIANS 3:7–9

But to each one of us grace has been given as Christ apportioned it.

—EPHESIANS 4:7

Grace to all who love our Lord Jesus Christ with an undying love.

—EPHESIANS 6:24

*It is right for me to feel this way about all of you, since I have you in my heart
and, whether I am in chains or defending and confirming the gospel, all of
you share in God's grace with me.*   —PHILIPPIANS 1:7

*In the same way, the gospel is bearing fruit and growing throughout the whole
world—just as it has been doing among you since the day you heard it and
truly understood God's grace.*   —COLOSSIANS 1:6

*Let your conversation be always full of grace, seasoned with salt, so that you
may know how to answer everyone.*   —COLOSSIANS 4:6

*I, Paul, write this greeting in my own hand. Remember my chains. Grace be
with you.*   —COLOSSIANS 4:18

*We pray this so that the name of our Lord Jesus may be glorified in you, and
you in him, according to the grace of our God and the Lord Jesus Christ.*

—2 THESSALONIANS 1:12

*May our Lord Jesus Christ himself and God our Father, who loved us and by
his grace gave us eternal encouragement and good hope, encourage your hearts
and strengthen you in every good deed and word.*

—2 THESSALONIANS 2:16–17

The grace of our Lord Jesus Christ be with you all.

—2 THESSALONIANS 3:18

The grace of our Lord was poured out on me abundantly, along with the faith and love that are in Christ Jesus.   —1 TIMOTHY 1:14

To Timothy, my dear son: Grace, mercy and peace from God the Father and Christ Jesus our Lord.   —2 TIMOTHY 1:2

He has saved us and called us to a holy life—not because of anything we have done but because of his own purpose and grace. This grace was given us in Christ Jesus before the beginning of time, but it has now been revealed through the appearing of our Savior, Christ Jesus, who has destroyed death and has brought life and immortality to light through the gospel.

—2 TIMOTHY 1:9–10

You then, my son, be strong in the grace that is in Christ Jesus.

—2 TIMOTHY 2:1

The Lord be with your spirit. Grace be with you all.   —2 TIMOTHY 4:22

For the grace of God has appeared that offers salvation to all people.

—TITUS 2:11

But when the kindness and love of God our Savior appeared, he saved us, not because of righteous things we had done, but because of his mercy. He saved us through the washing of rebirth and renewal by the Holy Spirit, whom he poured out on us generously through Jesus Christ our Savior, so that, having been justified by his grace, we might become heirs having the hope of eternal life.   —TITUS 3:4–7

But we do see Jesus, who was made lower than the angels for a little while, now crowned with glory and honor because he suffered death, so that by the grace of God he might taste death for everyone.   —HEBREWS 2:9

*Let us then approach God's throne of grace with confidence, so that we may
receive mercy and find grace to help us in our time of need.*

—HEBREWS 4:16

*How much more severely do you think someone deserves to be punished who
has trampled the Son of God underfoot, who has treated as an unholy thing
the blood of the covenant that sanctified them, and who has insulted the
Spirit of grace?*   —HEBREWS 10:29

*See to it that no one falls short of the grace of God and that no bitter root
grows up to cause trouble and defile many.*   —HEBREWS 12:15

*Do not be carried away by all kinds of strange teachings. It is good for our
hearts to be strengthened by grace, not by eating ceremonial foods, which is of
no benefit to those who do so.*   —HEBREWS 13:9

*But he gives us more grace. That is why Scripture says: "God opposes the
proud but shows favor to the humble."*   —JAMES 4:6

*Concerning this salvation, the prophets, who spoke of the grace that was to
come to you, searched intently and with the greatest care, trying to find out
the time and circumstances to which the Spirit of Christ in them was pointing
when he predicted the sufferings of the Messiah and the glories that would
follow.*   —1 PETER 1:10–11

*Therefore, with minds that are alert and fully sober, set your hope on the
grace to be brought to you when Jesus Christ is revealed at his coming.*

—1 PETER 1:13

*Each of you should use whatever gift you have received to serve others, as
faithful stewards of God's grace in its various forms.*   —1 PETER 4:10

*And the God of all grace, who called you to his eternal glory in Christ, after
you have suffered a little while, will himself restore you and make you strong,
firm and steadfast.*   —1 PETER 5:10

With the help of Silas, whom I regard as a faithful brother, I have written to you briefly, encouraging you and testifying that this is the true grace of God. Stand fast in it. —1 PETER 5:12

Grace and peace be yours in abundance through the knowledge of God and of Jesus our Lord. —2 PETER 1:2

But grow in the grace and knowledge of our Lord and Savior Jesus Christ. To him be glory both now and forever! Amen. —2 PETER 3:18

Helpful Books on Grace

- Blue, Ken, and Alden Swan. *The Gospel Uncensored.* WestBow Press, 2010.
- Bridges, Jerry. *The Discipline of Grace.* NavPress, 1994.
- Bridges, Jerry. *Transforming Grace.* NavPress, 2008.
- Falsani, Cathleen. *Sin Boldly: A Field Guide for Grace.* Zondervan, 2008.
- Jung, Joanne, J. *Knowing Grace.* Biblica, 2011.
- Lucado, Max. *Grace.* Thomas Nelson, 2012.
- Lucado, Max. *In the Grip of Grace.* Thomas Nelson, 1996.
- Manning, Brennan. *All is Grace.* David C. Cook, 2011.
- Manning, Brennan. *The Ragamuffin Gospel.* Multnomah, 1990.
- Oden, Thomas C. *The Transforming Power of Grace.* Abingdon Press, 1993.
- Palau, Andrew. *The Secret Life of a Fool.* Worthy, 2012.
- Smedes, Lewis B. *Shame and Grace.* HarperOne, 1993.
- Stanley, Andy. *The Grace of God.* Thomas Nelson, 2010.
- Swindoll, Charles. *The Grace Awakening.* Thomas Nelson, 1990.
- Taunton, Larry Alex. *The Grace Effect.* Thomas Nelson, 2011.
- Tchividjian, Tullian. *One Way Love.* David C. Cook, 2013.
- Wilder, Lynn K. *Unveiling Grace.* Zondervan, 2013.
- Wilhite, Jud, with Bill Taaffe. *Uncensored Grace.* Multnomah, 2009.
- Yancey, Philip. *Vanishing Grace.* Zondervan, 2014.
- Yancey, Philip. *What's So Amazing About Grace?* Zondervan, 1997.

Meet Lee Strobel

Atheist-turned-Christian Lee Strobel, the former award-winning legal editor of *The Chicago Tribune*, is a *New York Times* best-selling author of more than twenty books. He serves as Professor of Christian Thought at Houston Baptist University and as a teaching pastor at Woodlands Church in Texas.

Described in the *Washington Post* as "one of the evangelical community's most popular apologists," Lee shared the Christian Book of the Year award in 2005 for a curriculum he coauthored with Garry Poole about the movie *The Passion of the Christ*. He also won Gold Medallions for *The Case for Christ, The Case for Faith,* and *The Case for a Creator,* all of which have been made into documentaries distributed by Lionsgate.

His latest works include *The Case for Christianity Answer Book*; his first novel, *The Ambition*; and *The Case for Christ Study Bible,* which features hundreds of notes and articles. His free e-newsletter, *Investigating Faith,* is available at http://leestrobel.com/.

Lee was educated at the University of Missouri (Bachelor of Journalism degree) and Yale Law School (Master of Studies in Law degree). He was a journalist for fourteen years at the *Chicago Tribune* and other newspapers, winning Illinois' highest honor for public service journalism from United Press International. He also led a team that won UPI's top award for investigative reporting in Illinois.

After investigating the evidence for Jesus, Lee became a Christian in 1981. He joined the staff of Willow Creek Community Church in 1987 and later became a teaching pastor. He joined Saddleback Valley

Community Church as a teaching pastor in 2000. He left Saddle-back to write books and host the national network TV program *Faith Under Fire.*

In addition, Lee taught First Amendment law at Roosevelt University. In recognition of the extensive research for his books, he was honored by Southern Evangelical Seminary with the conferring of a Doctor of Divinity degree in 2007.

Lee's other books include *The Case for the Real Jesus, Finding the Real Jesus, God's Outrageous Claims, The Case for Christmas, The Case for Easter, The Unexpected Adventure* (coauthored with Mark Mittelberg), and *Surviving a Spiritual Mismatch in Marriage,* which he wrote with his wife, Leslie.

Lee also coauthored the *Becoming a Contagious Christian* course, which has trained a million-and-a-half Christians on how to naturally and effectively talk with others about Jesus.

He has been interviewed on such national TV networks as ABC, Fox, PBS, and CNN, and his articles have appeared in a variety of periodicals, including *The Christian Research Journal, Marriage Partnership, Discipleship Journal, Decision,* and the online editions of the *Wall Street Journal* and *Newsweek.* He has been a recurring guest on *The Bible Answer Man* and *Focus on the Family* radio programs. He is a member of the Evangelical Philosophical Society.

Lee and Leslie have been married for forty-two years and live in Texas. Their daughter, Alison, is the author of six novels and coauthor (with her husband Daniel) of two books for children. Their son, Kyle, has written several books on Jonathan Edwards and on spiritual formation. With a Ph.D. in theology from the University of Aberdeen and two master's degrees, he is a professor at the Talbot School of Theology at Biola University.

Acknowledgements

This book was a labor of love—but it was tough labor. By far, it was the most difficult book I have written, perhaps because it involved disclosing private matters about my personal life, family, and health that I had never shared publicly before.

My wife Leslie, children Alison and Kyle, and their spouses Dan and Kelli deserve my deep gratitude for having to endure me while I was in the throes of working on this project. They were constantly encouraging to me, even though I'm sure that wasn't always easy.

I'm thankful for my ministry partner for the last quarter of a century, Mark Mittelberg, who has been a faithful friend at all times. He is an endless source of ideas, affirmation, and input. As always, he read my first drafts—many of which were embarrassingly rough—and offered constructive and insightful feedback.

The team at Zondervan was exceedingly patient as this project blew past deadline after deadline. They gave me what I needed most—grace. I value my relationship with a company that has such integrity and vision.

I am especially thankful for my editor, John Sloan. As with all of my *Case* books, he guided me with his wisdom and creative genius. The trajectory he helped set at the beginning of this project was invaluable in keeping me on track. His patience, kindness, and consummate professionalism make him a joy to work with.

Most of all, I want to express my profound respect and appreciation for the people who allowed me to interview them for this book. I am so thankful for their honesty and vulnerability in teaching me more and more about God's grace.

Notes

Preface

1. Thomas C. Oden, *The Transforming Power of Grace* (Nashville: Abingdon), back cover.
2. Ibid., 33.
3. Ibid., 95.
4. Ibid.
5. "Quotes from Chuck Colson (1931 – 2012)," *The Poached Egg*, http://www.thepoachedegg.net/the-poached-egg/2012/04/quotes-from-chuck-colson-1931-2012.html.
6. Philip Yancey, "Grace," *Philip Yancey.com*, http://www.philipyancey.com/q-and-a-topics/grace.
7. Ibid.

INTRODUCTION: The Search for Grace

1. A. W. Tozer, *The Pursuit of God* (Camp Hill, PA: Wingspread, 2007), 17.

CHAPTER 1: The Mistake

1. Sigmund Freud, *Leonardo da Vinci* (New York: Vintage/Random House, 1947), 98.
2. See: Paul C. Vitz, *Faith of the Fatherless: The Psychology of Atheism* (Dallas: Spence, 1999). On p. 16 Vitz says, "Freud makes the simple and easily understandable claim that once a child or youth is disappointed in or loses respect for their earthly father, belief in a heavenly father becomes impossible. That a child's psychological representation of his father is intimately connected to his understanding of God was assumed by Freud and has been rather well developed by a number of psychologists, especially psychoanalysts. In other words, an atheist's disappointment in

and resentment of his own father unconsciously justifies his rejection of God." Many psychologists have stressed that the relationship between a child and his father is one factor among several that can influence his or her conception of God. Interestingly, research by Vern L. Bengtson of the University of Southern California at Santa Barbara found that for religious transmission through generations, "having a close bond with one's father matters even more than a close relationship with one's mother," except in Judaism. But he said, "Fervent faith cannot compensate for a distant dad." He found that "a father who is an exemplar, a pillar of the church, but doesn't provide warmth and affirmation to his kid does not have kids who follow him in his faith." See Mark Oppenheimer, "Book Explores Ways Faith is Kept, or Lost, Over Generations," *New York Times*, January 31, 2014, and Vern L. Bengtson with Norella M. Putney and Susan Harris, *Families and Faith: How Religion Is Passed Down across Generations* (New York: Oxford University Press, 2014).

3. See Charles Chandler, "From Disbelief to Devotion," *Decision*, March 2014.

CHAPTER 2: The Orphan

1. J. I. Packer, *Knowing God* (Downers Grove, IL: InterVarsity, 1973), 182, 194.

2. All interviews are edited for conciseness, clarity, and content. Stephanie Fast's website is http://www.stephaniefast.org/. She tells her story in her book *She Is Mine* (Aloha, OR.: D&S Publishing, 2014).

3. Paraphrase of a part of Psalm 10:14 KJV.

4. Packer, *Knowing God*, 182.

5. Ibid., 187–88.

6. Ibid., 196.

CHAPTER 3: The Addict

1. Douglas Wilson, "Bones and Silicon," *Blog & Mablog*, http://dougwils .com/s7-engaging-the-culture/bones-and-silicon.html.

2. Among the books in which he shares parts of his story are Jud Wilhite with Bill Taaffe, *Uncensored Grace* (Colorado Springs: Multnomah, 2008); Jud Wilhite, *Uncensored Truth* (Corona, CA: Ethur, 2010); Jud Wilhite, *Pursued: God's Divine Obsession with You* (New York: FaithWords, 2013); Jud Wilhite, *Throw It Down: Leaving Behind Behaviors*

and Dependencies That Hold You Back (Grand Rapids, MI: Zondervan, 2011); and Jud Wilhite, *The God of Yes* (New York: Faith Words, 2014).

3. See Tullian Tchividjian, *One Way Love: Inexhaustible Grace for an Exhausted World* (Colorado Springs: Cook, 2013).

4. Jerry Bridges, *Transforming Grace: Living Confidently in God's Unfailing Love* (Colorado Springs: NavPress, 1991), 9–10.

5. Walter Marshall and Bruce H. McRae, *The Gospel Mystery of Sanctification* (Eugene, OR: Wipf and Stock, 2004), 117.

6. See Ken Blue and Alden Swan, *The Gospel Uncensored* (Bloomington, IN: WestBow, 2010), 8–9. Blue describes how God renewed his faith through his study of Galatians.

7. "For through the law I died to the law so that I might live for God. I have been crucified with Christ and I no longer live, but Christ lives in me. The life I now live in the body, I live by faith in the Son of God, who loved me and gave himself for me" (Galatians 2:19–20).

8. Galatians 4:15 NIV 1984.

9. See Galatians 3:3.

10. See Galatians 5:1.

11. See Galatians 1:3 and 6:18.

12. Matthew 11:28.

13. See Stephanie Kishi, "Home of Sin City's Original Sin," *The Las Vegas Sun*, May 15, 2008.

14. "But the Pharisees and the teachers of the law muttered, 'This man welcomes sinners and eats with them'" (Luke 15:2).

15. See John 4:1–42.

16. C. S. Lewis, *Mere Christianity* (New York: Macmillan, 1960), 105–6.

17. See John 1:17.

18. See J. Murphy-O'Connor, "Corinth," *The Anchor Bible Dictionary*, Volume I. (New York: Doubleday, 1992), 1135–36. For a comparison of Corinth and Las Vegas, see Jud Wilhite with Bill Taaffe, *Uncensored Grace*, 68.

19. *Korinthiazesthai.*

20. See 1 Corinthians 1:3, 4.

21. "And if Christ has not been raised, your faith is futile; you are still in your sins" (1 Corinthians 15:17).

22. H. Richard Niebuhr, *The Kingdom of God in America* (New York: Harper & Row, 1959), 193.

CHAPTER 4: The Professor

1. Michka Assayas, *Bono: In Conversation with Michka Assayas* (New York: Riverhead, 2005), 204.

2. Ricky Gervais, "An (Atheist) Easter Message from Ricky Gervais," *The Wall Street Journal*, April 14, 2011.

3. "Simon Peter ... fell at Jesus's knees and said, 'Go away from me, Lord; I am a sinful man!'" (Luke 5:8). The use of *Lord* here connotes great respect; in this context, it does not acknowledge Jesus's divinity. See translator's note for this verse in *The NET Bible*, https://net.bible.org/#!bible/Luke+5.

4. See Luke 15:11–22.

5. See Gene Reeves, trans., *The Lotus Sutra: A Contemporary Translation of a Buddhist Classic* (Somerville, MA: Wisdom Publications, 2008), 142–45.

6. See John 4:1–26.

7. See Philip Yancey, *What's So Amazing About Grace?* (Grand Rapids, MI: Zondervan, 1997).

8. "Let those fight in the cause of Allah who sell the life of this world for the Hereafter. To him who fights in the cause of Allah—whether he is slain or gets victory—soon shall We give him a reward of great (value)" (Qur'an 4:74).

9. "... no bearer of burdens can bear the burden of another" (Qur'an 53:38).

10. Emphasis added.

11. The complete verse is: "For we labor diligently to write, to persuade our children, and also our brethren, to believe in Christ, and to be reconciled to God; for we know that it is by grace that we are saved, after all we can do" (2 Nephi 25:23).

12. "And now behold, my brethren, since it has been all that we could do (as we were the most lost of all mankind) to repent of all our sins and the many murders which we have committed, and to get God to take them away from our hearts, for it was all we could do to repent sufficiently before God that he would take away our stain" (Alma 24:11).

13. See Lucinda Dillon Kinkead and Dennis Romboy, "Deadly Taboo: Youth Suicide an Epidemic That Many in Utah Prefer to Ignore," *Deseret News*, April 24, 2006.

14. See Lee Strobel, *The Case for Faith* (Grand Rapids, MI: Zondervan, 2000), 25–55.

15. John 1:17.

16. See Mark Mittelberg, *Confident Faith: Building a Firm Foundation for Your Beliefs* (Carol Stream, IL: Tyndale, 2013).

CHAPTER 5: The Executioner

1. C. S. Lewis, *The Weight of Glory and Other Addresses* (New York: Collier/Macmillan, 1980), 125.

2. Nic Dunlop, *The Lost Executioner* (New York: Walker, 2006), 189.

3. David Chandler, *Voices from S-21* (Berkeley: University of California Press, 1999), vii.

4. Dunlop, *Lost Executioner*, 189.

5. Chandler, *Voices From S-21*, 3.

6. Dunlop, *Lost Executioner*, 19.

7. Chandler, *Voices from S-21*, 6.

8. Ibid., 77.

9. Dunlop, *Lost Executioner*, 23.

10. Duch's given name has been variously reported in articles and books. Christopher LaPel provided me with a photocopy of Duch's own writing, however, in which he clearly spells out his name as Kaing Guek Eav.

11. Seth Mydans, "'70's Torturer in Cambodia Now Doing God's Work,'" *New York Times*, May 2, 1999.

12. Mary Murphy, "Is There Anything God Can't Forgive?" *Purpose-Driven Magazine*, February 21, 2012.

13. Ibid.

14. See Dunlop, *Lost Executioner*, 254–62.

15. Ibid., 279, 254.

16. Ibid., 262.

17. Dunlop describes their meeting with Duch in Dunlop, *Lost Executioner*, 267–78. Thayer recounts the experience at "Nate Thayer Profile," *Nate Thayer*, http://natethayer.typepad.com.

18. Adrienne S. Gaines, "Notorious Cambodian Killer Seeks Forgiveness," *Charisma*, April 2, 1999.

19. Francois Bizot, "My Savior, Their Killer," *The New York Times*, February 17, 2009.

20. "Cambodia," *U.S. Department of State*, http://www.state.gov/j/drl/rls/irf/2010/148861.htm.

21. Murphy, "Is There Anything God Can't Forgive?"

22. Strobel, *Case for Faith*, 159.

23. "Will not the Judge of all the earth do right?" (Genesis 18:25).

CHAPTER 6: The Homeless

1. Yancey, *What's So Amazing About Grace?*, 70.

2. See http://brokenchainsoutreach.com/.

CHAPTER 7: The Pastor

1. Brennan Manning, *The Ragamuffin Gospel* (Colorado Springs: Multnomah, 2000), 26.

2. "Infidelity Statistics," *Statistics Brain*, http://www.statisticbrain.com/infidelity-statistics.

3. To avoid clues to the woman's identity, I have left out certain details of their relationship.

4. "Bear with each other and forgive one another if any of you has a grievance against someone. Forgive as the Lord forgave you" (Colossians 3:13).

5. 1 John 1:9.

6. "Moreover, we have all had human fathers who disciplined us and we respected them for it. How much more should we submit to the Father of spirits and live! They disciplined us for a little while as they thought best; but God disciplines us for our good, in order that we may share in his holiness. No discipline seems pleasant at the time, but painful. Later on, however, it produces a harvest of righteousness and peace for those who have been trained by it. Therefore, strengthen your feeble arms and weak knees. 'Make level paths for your feet,' so that the lame may not be disabled, but rather healed" (Hebrews 12:9-13).

7. See http://www.buildyourmarriage.org/.

CHAPTER 8: The Prodigal

1. Drew Dyck, *Yawning at Tigers* (Nashville: Nelson, 2014), 3.
2. See Luis Palau Association, http://www.palau.org/about/leadership/luispalau.
3. Proverbs 1:7; 1:32; 10:18; 10:21; 10:23; 12:23; 14:3; 14:8; 14:9; 15:5; 17:21; 23:9; 30:32.
4. Andrew Palau, *The Secret Life of a Fool* (Brentwood, TN: Worthy, 2012).
5. "For as he thinks within himself, so he is" (Proverbs 23:7 NASB).
6. Matthew 4:19.
7. See: Andrew Palau, *Secret Life of a Fool*, 85–88. For the story of Luis Palau's conversion, see Luis Palau, *Say Yes!* (Portland, OR: Multnomah, 1991), 31–34.
8. "The thief comes only to steal and kill and destroy; I came that they may have life, and have it abundantly" (Jesus, in John 10:10 NASB).
9. See Luke 18:18–29.
10. "He who began a good work in you will carry it on to completion until the day of Christ Jesus" (Philippians 1:6).
11. Dietrich Bonhoeffer, *The Cost of Discipleship* (New York: Touchstone, 1995), 44–45.
12. Ibid., 45.
13. Romans 12:1–2. Steve went on to read verse 3: "For by the grace given me I say to every one of you: Do not think of yourself more highly than you ought, but rather think of yourself with sober judgment, in accordance with the faith God has distributed to each of you."
14. See Isaiah 6.
15. See http://www.palau.org/.
16. "No one can come to me unless the Father who sent me draws them" (John 6:44). "He went on to say, 'This is why I told you that no one can come to me unless the Father has enabled them'" (John 6:65). Said theologian Thomas C. Oden: "Such drawing and enabling is precisely what is meant by prevenient grace...[which is] necessary for the very inception of faith." See Thomas C. Oden, *The Transforming Power of Grace*, 120. The Second Council of Orange in 529 said: "The sin of the first man has so impaired and weakened free will that no one thereafter can either love God as he ought or believe in God or do good for God's

sake, unless the grace of divine mercy has preceded him." See John Leith, ed., *Creeds of the Churches* (Richmond, VA: John Knox, 1979), 48.

17. John 1:12.

CHAPTER 9: Empty Hands

1. William Jurgens, *The Faith of the Early Fathers, Volume 3.* (Collegeville, MN: Liturgical Press, 1979), 44. The subtitle is part of the Augustine quotation.

2. John H. Coe is director of the Institute for Spiritual Formation at the Talbot School of Theology. The essentials of the prayer that Kyle took me through, and even some of the wording, were adapted from Coe's various writings. For instance, see John H. Coe, "Prayer of Recollection in Colossians," http://www.redeemerlm.org/uploads/1/2/0/7/12077040/prayer_of_recollection.pdf and also "Prayer of Recollection," *Wheat and Chaff,* http://wheat-chaff.org/spiritual-development/spiritual-formation/prayer-of-recollection.

EPILOGUE: Grace Withheld, Grace Extended

1. "Atheist-Illusionist Penn Jillette on Christians Who Don't Evangelize," *Preaching Today,* http://www.preachingtoday.com/illustrations/2009/may/2051109.html.

2. "For, 'Everyone who calls on the name of the Lord will be saved.' How, then, can they call on the one they have not believed in? And how can they believe in the one of whom they have not heard? And how can they hear without someone preaching to them? And how can anyone preach unless they are sent? As it is written: 'How beautiful are the feet of those who bring good news!'" (Romans 10:13–15).

3. Max Lucado, *Grace* (Nashville: Nelson, 2012), 192, citing Matthew 10:8.

4. Acts 10:24, *The Message.*

WILLOW CREEK ASSOCIATION

This resource is just one of many ministry tools published in partnership with the Willow Creek Association. Founded in 1992, WCA was created to serve churches and church leaders striving to create environments where those still outside the family of God are welcomed—and can more easily consider God's loving offer of salvation through faith.

These innovative churches and leaders are connected at the deepest level by their all-out dedication to Christ and His Kingdom. Willing to do whatever it required to build churches that help people move along the path toward Christ-centered devotion; they also share a deep desire to encourage all believers at every step of their faith journey, to continue moving toward a fully transformed, Christ-centered life.

Today, more than 10,000 churches from 80 denominations worldwide are formally connected to WCA and each other through WCA Membership. Many thousands more come to WCA for networking, training, and resources.

For more information about the ministry of the
Willow Creek Association, visit: **willowcreek.com**.

The Case for Christ

A Journalist's Personal Investigation of the Evidence for Jesus

Lee Strobel, New York Times Bestselling Author

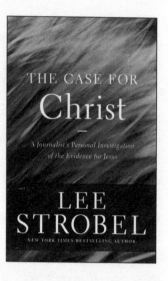

Is there credible evidence that Jesus of Nazareth really is the Son of God? Retracing his own spiritual journey from atheism to faith, Lee Strobel, former legal editor of the *Chicago Tribune*, cross-examines a dozen experts with doctorates from schools like Cambridge, Princeton, and Brandeis who are recognized authorities in their fields. Strobel challenges them with questions like: How reliable is the New Testament? Does evidence for Jesus exist outside the Bible? Is there any reason to believe the resurrection was an actual event? Strobel's tough, point-blank questions make this award-winning book read like a captivating, fast-paced novel. But it's not fiction. It's a riveting quest for the truth about history's most compelling figure. What will your verdict be in *The Case for Christ*?

"Lee Strobel probes with bulldog-like tenacity the evidence for the truth of biblical Christianity."—Bruce M. Metzger, Ph.D., Professor of New Testament, Emeritus, Princeton Theological Seminary

"Lee Strobel asks the questions a tough-minded skeptic would ask. His book is so good I read it out loud to my wife evenings after dinner. Every inquirer should have it."—Phillip E. Johnson, Law Professor, University of California at Berkeley

Available in stores and online!

The Case for Faith

A Journalist Investigates the Toughest Objections to Christianity

Lee Strobel, New York Times Bestselling Author

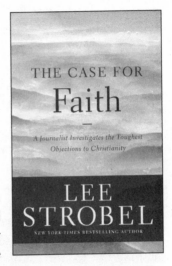

Was God telling the truth when he said, "You will seek me and find me when you seek me with all your heart"? In his #1 bestseller *The Case for Christ*, Lee Strobel examined the claims of Christ, reaching the hard-won verdict that Jesus is God's unique son. In *The Case for Faith*, Strobel turns his skills to the most persistent emotional objections to belief—the eight "heart barriers" to faith. This Gold Medallion-winning book is for those who may be feeling attracted to Jesus but who are faced with difficult questions standing squarely in their path. For Christians, it will deepen their convictions and give them fresh confidence in discussing Christianity with even their most skeptical friends.

"Everyone—seekers, doubters, fervent believers—benefits when Lee Strobel hits the road in search of answers, as he does again in *The Case for Faith*. In the course of his probing interviews, some of the toughest intellectual obstacles to faith fall away."—Luis Palau, evangelist, radio host, speaker, bestselling author.

Available in stores and online!

The Case for a Creator

A Journalist Investigates Scientific Evidence That Points Toward God

Lee Strobel, New York Times Bestselling Author

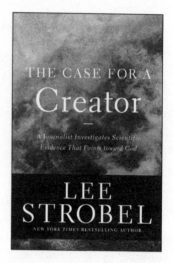

"My road to atheism was paved by science ... but, ironically, so was my later journey to God."—Lee Strobel

During his academic years, Lee Strobel became convinced that God was outmoded, a belief that colored his ensuing career as an award-winning journalist at the *Chicago Tribune*. Science had made the idea of a Creator irrelevant—or so Strobel thought. But today science is pointing in a different direction. In recent years, a diverse and impressive body of research has increasingly supported the conclusion that the universe was intelligently designed. At the same time, Darwinism has faltered in the face of concrete facts and hard reason. Has science discovered God? At the very least, it's giving faith an immense boost as new findings emerge about the incredible complexity of our universe. Join Strobel as he reexamines the theories that once led him away from God. Through his compelling and highly readable account, you'll encounter the mind-stretching discoveries from cosmology, cellular biology, DNA research, astronomy, physics, and human consciousness that present astonishing evidence in *The Case for a Creator*. Mass market edition available in packs of six.

Available in stores and online!

ZONDERVAN®
.com

The Case for the Real Jesus

A Journalist Investigates Current Attacks on the Identity of Christ

Lee Strobel, New York Times Bestselling Author

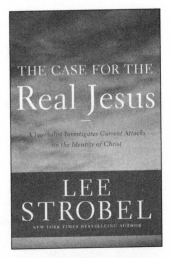

Has modern scholarship debunked the traditional Christ? Has the church suppressed the truth about Jesus to advance its own agenda? What if the real Jesus is far different from the atoning Savior worshiped through the centuries? In *The Case for the Real Jesus,* former award-winning legal editor Lee Strobel explores such hot-button questions as: Did the church suppress ancient non-biblical documents that paint a more accurate picture of Jesus than the four Gospels? Did the church distort the truth about Jesus by tampering with early New Testament texts? Do new insights and explanations finally disprove the resurrection? Have fresh arguments disqualified Jesus from being the Messiah? Did Christianity steal its core ideas from earlier mythology? Evaluate the arguments and evidence being advanced by prominent atheists, liberal theologians, Muslim scholars, and others. Sift through expert testimony. Then reach your own verdict in *The Case for the Real Jesus.*

Available in stores and online!

The Case for Christ Study Guide with DVD

A Six-Session Investigation of the Evidence for Jesus

Lee Strobel, New York Times Bestselling Author

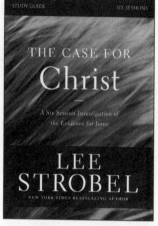

Is there credible evidence that Jesus of Nazareth really is the Son of God? Skeptics dismiss the Jesus of the Gospels by claiming there is no evidence in the case for Christ. Lee Strobel disagrees. The former legal journalist and one-time atheist knows how to ask tough questions. His own search for truth about Jesus led him to faith in Christ.

Now Strobel invites you and your group to investigate the truth about Jesus Christ leading to the facts that guided Strobel from atheism to faith in Christ.

In this revised six-session video study, participants will journey along with Strobel on a quest for the truth about Jesus. Rejecting easy answers, you will sift through fascinating historical evidence as you weigh compelling expert testimony. In the end, groups may very well see Jesus in a new way—and even, like Strobel, find their life transformed.

Pastors, small group leaders, and individuals will find compelling answers for their questions about Jesus in The Case for Christ Revised: A DVD Study. This package—perfect for small groups and Bible studies—includes one study guide and one DVD.

The six sessions include: The Investigation of a Lifetime; Eyewitness Evidence; Evidence Outside the Bible; Analyzing Jesus; Evidence for the Resurrection; and Reaching Your Verdict.

Available in stores and online!